GOOD NEWS, BAD NEWS

FATHER C. JOHN McCLOSKEY III
AND
RUSSELL SHAW

GOOD NEWS, BAD NEWS

Evangelization, Conversion, and the Crisis of Faith

IGNATIUS PRESS SAN FRANCISCO

Cover design by John Herreid

ISBN 978-1-58617-125-4
ISBN 1-58617-125-9
Library of Congress Control Number 2006924090
Printed in the United States of America ♾

DEDICATION

This book is dedicated to my parents, my brother,
and my sisters, who formed and
accompanied me in my early growth in the faith.
It also is dedicated to my spiritual family,
Opus Dei, which continues to call
me to a deeper conversion to Christ.

CJM III

CONTENTS

ACKNOWLEDGMENTS

No one writes a book alone. Everyone who writes a book is obliged to share much of the praise for the results, but none of the blame, with many people who helped him on the journey.

I wish to acknowledge the kindness of Peter Brown, director of the Netherhall International Residence in Hampstead, London, who allowed me the use of the library and computer room, where I spent many hours. Thanks also to Dr. John Henry, Father Gerard Sheehan, and the residents of Rutland, who provided "family" life and suffered my colonial idiosyncracies with much patience.

Starting at the start, I am grateful to the Sisters of Charity who taught me at St. Jane de Chantal School in Bethesda, Maryland, and to the Christian Brothers and excellent lay faculty at St. John's College High School in Washington, D.C. Such order and discipline as I possess have a lot to do with my participation there in Junior ROTC.

Thanks to my fellow students and my professors at Columbia College in New York, where I enjoyed what I regard as the finest liberal arts program in the United States. Thanks to my co-workers and supervisors at Citibank and Merrill Lynch in New York, where I learned to count and sell—and also to deal (cordially, I hope) with people of what may be a greater variety of races, colors, and creeds than can be found even in London. The experience has been immensely helpful in my pastoral work.

Thanks to the students at Princeton University, where I spent some very interesting and challenging years as a chaplain. By now they are well along in raising their families and pursuing their careers and thereby evangelizing the world. Some are priests and religious. In a special way, I want to thank Father Charles Weiser, who welcomed me to the Aquinas Institute at Princeton as a fellow priest interested only in the glory of God and the salvation of souls.

Thanks to the board, staff, and congregation of the Catholic Information Center of the Archdiocese of Washington, where I spent several years as director. What a thrill it was to return to my hometown—ten blocks from where I was born and a three-minute walk from the White House! Twice all of us moved the Center to new locations in downtown Washington, including its present site, 1501 K Street NW, where it provides a unique service in the nation's capital to many thousands who pass through its doors each year. I ask your prayers for the late James Cardinal Hickey of Washington, who first arranged for a priest of Opus Dei to be the Center's director. Special thanks also to Dennis Bolster, Helena Metzger, and Veronica Conkling, who did so much to make the CIC not only an apostolate but also a home.

I express heartfelt gratitude to Peter Kleponis, M.A., L.P.C., and Richard Fitzgibbons, M.D. By showing me the value of letting go of excessive responsibility, they helped me resolve serious health issues during a difficult period of my life; thanks to their help and God's grace, my future looks brighter and more productive than ever. I am grateful, too, to Lewis and Thomas Lehrman, father and son, and the Lehrman Institute, good friends and sources of assistance for various projects; and to Dr. Robert Royal, president of the Faith and Reason Institute and a cherished friend.

Thanks, finally, to the converts whose stories fill and enliven the pages of this book. I was overwhelmed—

moved to tears, I'm not ashamed to say—by the generosity of their response to my invitation to share their recollections and their insights. Not all of the stories they provided are here verbatim, but all are present in this book in one way or another. In no special order they are: Ann English, Alex and Pegie Morris, Alfred S. Regnery, John Steele, Matt Ando, Jamie James, Austin Ruse, Brian Robertson, Tim Carney, Tom Carr, Father Carter Griffin, Cindy Searcy, Darla Romfo, David Wagner, Diane Brynn, David Gersten, Dr. Bernard Nathanson, Doug Branch, Ed Hadas, Chris Dixon, Lee Edwards, Lewis Lehrman, Erica Walter, Father John Saward, Bob Novak, Tom Farr, Father David L. Stokes, Garret and Robert Morris, George Khalsa, Larry Kudlow, Harry Crocker, Jeff Bell, Patricia Ireland, Jason Boffetti, Jack Bluestein, Mark Belnick, Capt. Jeffrey Townsend, Jim Morgan, Jeff Finch, Sen. Sam Brownback, Jennifer Ferrara, Kathleen Dezio, Lou Carlin, Laura McPherson, Tom Pyle, Meghan Gurdon, Michael Woodward, Deacon Michael Ross, Melissa Stass, Kyle Parker, Carlie Dixon, Dave Phelps, Paul (Chaim) Schenck, Robert Traynham, Ruth Belmonte, Susan Collins, Scott Walter, Steve Warner, Sister Mary Odo (Jenny Tilley) and her mother Kathy, Tony Snow, Brad Wilcox, Paul Corzine, Dave Branyan, Bill Saunders, Bill Park, Sandi McCloskey, Adam and Kathy Carlisle, Judge Robert Bork, Robin Harriss, Robert Spencer, Sister Maris Stella of Jesus Crucified (Leila Bate), Rado Nickolov, David Leonard, Mark Polonski, Tony Aragon, and David Clark.

I wish there were many more names, and I pray God will give me many more years to bring him souls. If he doesn't, you the reader will just have to work twice as hard.

Rev. C. John McCloskey III

INTRODUCTION

by Russell Shaw

"Good news and bad news", said the agent at the airline check-in counter in Munich.

I cringed.

"The good news", she went on, "is that the flight to Dulles is on time. The bad news is that it's a full flight. I put you in a middle seat."

A short time later, fearing the worst—a 350-pound woman on one side of me, a man with a hacking cough on the other—I boarded the plane. Traveling by way of Munich, I was heading back to the United States after two weeks in Rome spent lecturing at a university and attending a meeting at the Vatican.

The 350-pound woman and the coughing man apparently missed the plane. What I got instead were a quiet young chap in his late twenties on my left and, on my right, a blonde young woman, twenty at most, in tee shirt and jeans. Breathing a sigh of relief, I settled in for the nine-hour flight.

I'd planned on a nap after lunch, but my seatmate to the right had other ideas. Her name was Caitlin. She was friendly and wanted to talk.

She was a junior at a Lutheran college in the Midwest, returning home from a week-long spring break spent in Rome with friends and classmates. She said she was studying Far Eastern culture and foreign languages.

I asked, "What do you want to be?"

The answer was a surprise: "A missionary."

She wasn't kidding. Blonde, chatty Caitlin looked and acted like the all-American girl, but as she talked it became clear that the great passion of her life was the good news of Christ. And some of what she said about that was more than a little disconcerting to me, a lifelong Roman Catholic.

I asked her where she had it in mind to be a missionary. Thinking of her Far Eastern studies, I supposed she would name some country like Korea or Japan. I was wrong. She thought Rome looked like a pretty good place to preach Christ.

During her spring break, it turned out, she'd pretty much skipped the usual tourist sights—the Colosseum, the Trevi Fountain, the Spanish Steps, and the rest—and spent her time evangelizing other students in the hostel where she and her friends were staying.

The Italian university students in particular intrigued her. "They were all baptized as Catholics," she explained, "but they said they'd had Catholicism crammed down their throats, and they were sick of it by now. I think Rome would be a great place to make converts to *real* Christianity. Excuse me for asking, by the way, but ... what religion are you?"

"I'm a practicing Roman Catholic."

"Oh! I didn't mean to offend you." Caitlin was nonplussed—although not very.

"I'm not offended", I assured her. "There's a lot of truth in what you say. But of course it's only part of the truth and not the whole of it."

I went on to discourse knowledgeably about the problems of alienation and loss of faith that could occur when superficial cultural Catholicism—or a merely "cultural" brand of any religion—found itself facing the challenge of secularism and a culture without faith. Mischievously, considering her Lutheran roots, I suggested to Caitlin that if she was looking for a *really* post-Christian setting in which to be a missionary, modern-day Scandinavia would suit her just fine. (I'm not sure she got the point: innocence is sometimes its own best defense.)

"Anyway," I wound up, "the story has another, more positive side. A lot of Christians today have recognized the problem you recognized and are working to interiorize and deepen their faith. There are a lot of good things going on, actually, in the Catholic Church, in Rome and everywhere else. Alongside much that's still pretty bad."

For some time, the young man on my left had been listening in. Back before lunch he'd introduced himself as Josh and said he was an environmental consultant who lived in Vermont and was going home after several weeks of consulting in Poland. Caitlin looked across me to him. "Are you a Christian?" she asked cheerfully.

Josh hesitated. "I guess you could say I'm on the sidelines watching the game", he answered. "It's like I'm making up my mind whether I want to play."

Caitlin and I absorbed that but said nothing. The conversation went on. Now she had a question for me: "What do Catholics *really* believe about Mary? You hear so many different things. And what about the Rosary? Tell me about that."

Stumbling and fumbling, I tried to give a thumbnail account of Catholic doctrine and devotion regarding the Blessed Virgin. "Tremendously important in God's plan . . . model and intercessor for us all . . . our mother in a real, spiritual sense . . . but we don't worship her, if that's what you mean . . . what she mainly does is lead us to Christ."

The Rosary was easier. I had mine in my pocket, and I pulled it out and showed it to the two young people—wooden beads on a thick cord. "Good for going through security at the airport", I pointed out.

Then I told them what I could about the Rosary: the sets of mysteries ("important events in the lives of Jesus and Mary", I translated); a simple, practical way to combine vocal prayer and meditation; a good way of praying when you were too tired or too busy to do anything else. "I often say the Rosary when I'm driving", I told them.

Josh hadn't said much up to then. Now he volunteered an unexpected statement that surprised Caitlin and me: "I've made pilgrimages with a friend of mine." It turned out that he'd been to Lourdes, Fatima, Santiago de Compostela, Medjugorje. In Poland he had visited Czestochowa.

This sounded like something more than watching from the sidelines. "I guess I'm kind of searching", he admitted sheepishly. Then, "My Catholic grandmother would be pleased."

I felt that I should say something inspiring to get him off the sidelines and into the game. Caitlin, too—she needed a word of advice that would provide some direction for her enthusiasm and idealism. Nothing came to mind. The conversation had played itself out. Soon Caitlin was hopping out of her seat to visit her friends at the back of the plane. Josh read a magazine. I took my nap.

It seemed like only a short time before we were circling Dulles Airport in Northern Virginia outside Washington, D.C. When we had landed and were preparing to debark, I told Caitlin I would pray for her and asked her to pray for me. I wished Josh good luck. They vanished up the aisles on either side of the plane as I struggled to get a piece of luggage out of the overhead rack.

Waiting in line at passport control with passengers from your own flight and several others is a terrific opportunity for introspection. In our own particular ways, I thought, each of us is searching. I suspect Josh may be closer than he thinks. Caitlin is sure she's found Jesus, but he may have some surprises in store for her. And me? For me, like everybody else, God's will unfolds neither more nor less than one day at a time.

A Specialist at Work

Father C. John McCloskey III has done more than most people to help others on their spiritual journeys. Profiling Father McCloskey in his book *Priest* (Sophia Institute Press, 2003), journalist Michael S. Rose called him "a 'specialist' in the business of transforming souls". Rose wrote:

> As a specialist, he eschews the more institutional approach to conversion that has unfortunately become the order of the day. "Many people are turned off by the bureaucratic approach that says, 'Hey, if you want to be a Catholic, you have to come here every Tuesday night for a year', or even worse, 'Sorry, our convert program started in late August. So you'll have to wait for next year.' ... I tailor-make my approach to the individual, considering his circumstances, and try to find out what's best for him."

He's had some notable successes. The list of those he has helped find their way into the Church includes prominent figures like onetime abortionist and proabortion activist Dr. Bernard Nathanson, Kansas Republican Senator Sam Brownback, Wall Street analyst Lawrence Kudlow, syndicated political columnist Robert Novak, and publisher Alfred S. Regnery. But these are just the iceberg's tip. Beyond the familiar names are hundreds of less well-known men and women who share something in common: "Father John" helped them to become Catholics.

C. John McCloskey III is a native of Washington, D.C., where he attended St. John's College High School. It's unquestionably a miracle of reconciling grace that he and I have been able to collaborate on a book, considering that from time immemorial St. John's, conducted by the Christian Brothers, has been the hated rival of my Jesuit high school, Gonzaga. We called the men of St. John's Johnnymops; heaven knows what they called us. While there, at the age of sixteen he joined the predominantly lay Catholic group Opus Dei.

After attending Columbia University, Father McCloskey worked on Wall Street. Discerning still another bend on his vocational path, he next headed for Rome, where he studied for the priesthood at the Roman College of the Holy Cross, the formation center for priests of Opus Dei. Ordained in 1982, he returned to the United States to do pastoral work with Opus Dei in New York. In 1985 he started traveling three days a week to Princeton University, where he served as a chaplain—unofficial at first, then official, then unofficial again—to Catholic students.

That needs explaining. No one has ever accused Father McCloskey of not speaking his mind, and in due course he became a controversial figure in some Princeton circles for his outspoken views about the politically correct, anti-Christian paganism that he found perverting students on this distinguished campus.

Michael Rose calls it "ironic" that some members of the Princeton community wanted the priest suppressed for what he said: "They accused him of wanting to stamp out those who disagreed with him, yet they tried to silence him by demanding his expulsion." In 1990 the chief Catholic chaplain, reacting to the controversy, dismissed him as an assistant. He continued his ministry to students at the Opus Dei center in Princeton until 1998.

Then he was transferred to Washington to assume the directorship of the Catholic Information Center—the CIC for short. This was a downtown institution dating back to the 1950s whose operation the Archbishop of Washington had turned over several years earlier to Opus Dei.

Located a five-minute walk from the White House, on the K Street power corridor, close to government agencies, high-priced legal and lobbying firms, private clubs, hotels, and glittering shops of every kind, the CIC serves a varied clientele made up of professionals, workers, tourists, and passersby as a kind of midtown daytime "parish" at the center of the action in the heart of the nation's capital. For more than five years it was a congenial environment for Father John—a base well suited to his diversified ministry, including the convert making that is the substance of this book.

What does a specialist in evangelization and convert making do? Although the book isn't an autobiography, it contains an implicit answer to that.

The most important thing about conversion is, of course, that it's God's work and God's alone. Others, including the converts themselves, only respond to divine initiatives, only cooperate with grace.

Still, there are steps to be taken, things that work and things that don't, certain patterns that tend to repeat themselves. It is important, too, to have a solid grasp of the present religious and cultural situation, the contemporary context for the operation of grace, as well as some knowledge of the living continuity of past and present—the tradition—from which Catholics draw their spiritual sustenance in and through the Church. A "specialist" in the business of transforming souls here explains all this.

A Word about This Book

The book is Father C. John McCloskey's, but I had more than a small hand in it, too, in several ways: by organizing material he provided me (mainly articles of his and answers to questions I put to him to draw him out on matters that needed clarifying), rewriting for clarity and style, here and there adding thoughts of my own that seemed congruent with something he'd said. The results are authentic McCloskey, yet not entirely without Shaw. A collaboration, in other words, in which each collaborator brought something important to the finished product.

One of my most useful contributions may have been the following. As I was preparing to begin the writing of the book, I explained to Father John that we badly needed something lacking up to that point. "Your theory of evangelization and conversion is excellent," I told him, "but theory isn't enough. We need case histories, personal examples, the human dimension."

Thinking that over, he had a marvelous idea. He e-mailed a number of people whom he'd helped bring into the Church and told them, "What I am asking from you is very simple. Write a paragraph or two or three about what most strongly attracted you to the Church and also about what were your greatest difficulties. And if I had any role in your conversion, mention what I said or what arguments I used that you found helpful in understanding the faith better."

The responses were swift in coming and remarkably generous. The experiences and insights provided by these several dozen men and women leaven the book and help make it much more exciting—and more useful—than it otherwise would have been. Going far beyond "a paragraph or two or three", many wrote short, moving autobiographical essays that display extraordinary perception regarding the workings of grace and the dynamics of the spiritual life.

Gobbledygook or Good News?

These are matters where straight talk is badly needed.

Not long ago I came across a prominent churchman's account of who Jesus is and the role he plays in our lives: "For young people struggling with uncertainty created by the contemporary cultural attitude, the challenge must be addressed by the knowledge of Christ as the historically lived and contemporary presence of the revelation of God in his Easter mystery of death and Resurrection."

Huh? Simply as rhetoric, that's rather thin gruel by comparison with, say, the great organ chords that open Gerard Manley Hopkins' *The Wreck of the Deutschland*:

> Thou mastering me
> God! giver of breath and bread;
> World's strand, sway of the sea;
> Lord of living and dead. . . .

And not much nourishment either for people starved for something—Someone—to believe in.

Such people will find help and inspiration in sentiments expressed by a woman whom Father John baptized and confirmed in May 2002. Near the end of a narrative that runs thirteen single-spaced pages, she writes:

> I know this is too much for you, Father, but I am still so overwhelmed by the grace that brought me to you and has led me to such joy in my life, joy that I never knew was possible. I'm still the same person, with all the same failings, all the same difficulties, all the same challenges, all the same tendencies, and yet I'm an entirely different person because I see everything in the light of Christ, understanding that ultimately I can handle anything that comes from him. . . . I'm looking at everything and asking, what is it God is showing me, what is he asking of me, what does he want me to do so that I can become stronger, even in the most mundane things? I am thrilled to be a child of God and am becoming more of an adult toward the world because

> I am allowing myself to be that child. So often I stop and marvel at the fact that God loves me. How unbelievable that is!
>
> And at the same time how sure I am that it is true. I revel in the paradoxes.

"I revel in the paradoxes." Or, as C. S. Lewis put it in the title of his conversion story, Surprised by Joy.

When I got home from Dulles Airport after that trip from Rome via Munich, I found waiting for me the first batch of Father John's raw material for this book. Too bad I hadn't read it before I ran into Caitlin and Josh—I might have had a better idea what to say to them. But not to worry—there will be other occasions, other Caitlins and other Joshes, for sure. We are all called to be evangelizers, whenever and however God wants. "Always be prepared to make a defense to any one who calls you to account for the hope that is in you" (1 Pet 3:15). But be sure to do it, the epistle adds, "with gentleness and reverence".

And as Pope John Paul II reminds us in *Novo Millennio Ineunte* (At the Start of the New Millennium):

> It is not therefore a matter of inventing a new program. The program already exists: it is the plan found in the gospel and in the living tradition, it is the same as ever. Ultimately, it has its center in Christ himself, who is to be known, loved and imitated, so that in him we may live the life of the Trinity, and with him transform history until its fulfillment in the heavenly Jerusalem.

I

Doing as the Romans Did

Many Americans would be happy to forget September 11, 2001, if they could, but the horror and outrage of that day are indelibly stamped on their memories. And so is something else. Amid the carnage of the terrorist attacks on the World Trade Center and the Pentagon, millions felt a sudden need for prayer. One of them was a woman living and working in Washington whom I'll call Marsha.

The daughter of secular Jews ("The big joke in my family was that I didn't know who Moses was"), she was married to a nonpracticing Catholic named Chris and had some good Catholic friends, but where religion was concerned that was as far as it went. Then came 9/11. Let her tell the story.

"It was the moment when I was finally awakened to my need for God. President Bush called for Americans to pray together at noon on Friday, September 14. Typically, the agency where I worked as an economist wouldn't participate in anything that might smack of Christianity, for fear of offending non-Christians and atheists. They decided instead to offer what sounded like a group hug in a big hall at 2 P.M.

"I was disgusted. I wanted a place where I could be with others who were praying at noon. The only church I could think of was a nearby Catholic church, so I went there.

"It was packed. I squeezed into a middle pew. I didn't understand much of the Mass, but I was well aware that I was surrounded by people who'd come there to pray. The priest's homily made a deep impression. He was a visitor from Northern Ireland, and he provided a perspective on what it means to live under the shadow of terrorism. By the end of the service, along with feeling deep sorrow, I felt fortunate."

A month later Marsha told Chris that she thought she wanted to become a Catholic. He phoned an old family friend, now a priest who lived in Rome but just then was in Boston giving a retreat. He told her to go see me at the Catholic Information Center in Washington—and she did. Early in the new year Chris returned to the Church. On May 18, 2002, Marsha was baptized, confirmed, and married, and received her First Communion, all in about thirty minutes.

"I was never so happy as that day," she recalls, "and I remember telling you how extraordinary it was to take communion at last, and you spoke about Communion as coming together in an incomparable way with God . . . in such a complete, loving way. That was the first time I experienced it. Since then I have experienced it in so many different ways!"

In case you wonder, this almost intuitive sense of the centrality of the Mass and Communion is far from being uncommon among prospective Catholics. Another woman, formerly an Evangelical Protestant and now an enthusiastic Catholic, says that when she was looking into the Church, she quickly realized that if she could settle "the issue of the Eucharist", then "eventually all the other things—the infallibility of the Pope, praying to Mary and the saints, and the rest—would fall into place. And they did." When you think about what Mass and Communion are, that stands to reason.

A Real "Age of the Laity"

Admit it. Don't you sometimes think how terrific it would be to share the joy in your heart that comes from the fullness of Catholic faith with your neighbor, your friend, a family member, a colleague at work? You'd hardly be reading this book if you didn't. Perhaps you've already had the wonderful experience of being godparent of someone you helped bring into the Church. If so, you know the special joy that fills a person's heart at being God's instrument.

The joy has always been there, of course, but it's especially intense today. For we are surrounded by a culture of death in which many people find little or no real meaning in their lives. Throughout the entire Christian era up to now, has there ever been a more lonely and profoundly clueless society than ours? This is a society that appears to have gained the whole world while forgetting the very existence of its own soul.

In a real sense, nonetheless, we've been here before. The steady growth of the infant Church in the first three centuries took place in the setting of a society anything but friendly to Christianity and sometimes actively hostile. To a great extent, the expansion came about through the good example and personal influence of thousands of Christian lay people.

Then, following the official acceptance of Christianity by the Roman Empire early in the fourth century, the living out of Christian ideals in the world gradually transformed the West into the Christian culture of the Middle Ages. Christendom lasted a millennium, but in the modern era it collapsed under the impact of events like the Reformation and the Enlightenment and ideas and ideologies like Darwinism, Marxism, and Freudianism.

So now we face the need to do again what our forebears in the faith did all those centuries ago—I mean evangelize a largely pagan society and convert the pagans. And, just as it was back then, "we" here means you, the Catholic laity, who during the last several centuries have so often been apostolically AWOL—content, that is, to let the clergy and religious do the heavy lifting of evangelization and winning converts to our one, holy, apostolic Catholic Church.

Time and again this has been called the "age of the laity". It's a beautiful thought. But the success of a *real* age of the laity, whenever one finally arrives, won't be measured by how many lay people get involved in lay ministries, as commendable as such involvement often is. It will be measured by quantitative and qualitative growth in the intensity of prayer, sacramental participation, and apostolic fervor on the part of the laity.

And as that kind of growth takes place, it will lead inevitably to the transformation of the contemporary culture into one that faithfully reflects Christ's teaching as mediated by the Church.

"Primarily through her laity," Pope John Paul II told the American bishops in 1987, "the Church is in a position to exercise great influence upon American culture." Then he asked, "But how is American culture evolving today? Is the evolution being influenced by the Gospel? Does it clearly reflect Christian inspiration? Your music, your poetry and art, your drama, your painting and sculpture, the literature that you are producing—are all those things which reflect the soul of a nation being influenced by the spirit of Christ for the perfection of humanity?"

Decades may have to pass before the answer to that question is an unqualified yes, but the changes that are necessary really can happen. Obviously, though, they will not happen by themselves, and the powerful forces of secularism are bent on seeing that they don't happen at all. The process of making them happen must start with the personal conversion of each one of us. That will lead to the conversion of many others.

Call It *Apostolate*, Please

You can call this sharing of the faith by a variety of names—evangelization, giving witness, proclaiming the good news, and others. I like the word *apostolate*.

"The individual apostolate," says the Second Vatican Council, "flowing generously from its source in a truly Christian life, is the origin and condition of the whole lay apostolate. . . . Regardless of status, all lay persons (including those who have no opportunity or possibility for collaboration in associations) are called to this type of apostolate and obliged to engage in it."

When Vatican Council II talks about the role of the laity, it doesn't spend a whole lot of time talking about what lay men and women should be doing inside the Church. The Council allows for lay ministries, but it doesn't put the emphasis on them. Instead it concentrates on what lay people ought to be doing out in the world. Essentially, that comes down to two things: seeking holiness and extending the kingdom of God on earth through family life, friendship, work, study—in a word, through apostolate.

The words and example of good friends can hardly be exaggerated.

"When I interned in D.C.," recalls Randy, one of the converts whom I was privileged to help, "some of my fellow interns encouraged me to come to church, and I was open to it, partly because thinking about things like death and marriage was starting to make me search for a real purpose to life."

"Chris and I spent many Friday evenings at an Irish bar near Capitol Hill, talking with John. After a drink had softened my inhibitions and maybe made me forget my manners, I would challenge him to explain to me how God could exist", recalls Marsha, the woman quoted above. Note that John—by now a priest—was the person whom she called when she decided to become a Catholic.

And here's a young man named Gus, recalling fellows at his Ivy League university: "Dave and other Catholics seemed persons leading lives worthy of emulation—lives that appeared not to be meaningless like mine."

The name for what Dave and John and the rest were doing isn't proselytism (in its popular, pejorative sense). It has absolutely nothing to do with coercion or lack of respect for the freedom of others. Only God's grace can effect a conversion. Pressure (other than the "pressure" brought to bear through prayer, sacrifice, good example, and friendship) simply doesn't work.

"Making" Converts: The Early Christians

So what does work? Excuse the repetition, but let me say it again: *we* don't make converts; *God* does. But each of us, potentially, has a role to play in it. To get some notion of that, let's take a closer look at those Christians of the Roman Empire.

"How was it done?" asks Rodney Stark, a distinguished sociologist of religion, in his book *The Rise of Christianity* (Princeton University Press, 1996). "How did a tiny and obscure messianic movement from the edge of the Roman Empire dislodge classical paganism and become the dominant faith of Western civilization?"

In raising this question, Stark is looking for the natural and human explanations of the phenomenon, not the supernatural ones. A Christian would certainly, and rightly, see the conversion of pagan Rome as clear evidence of the activity of the Holy Spirit, whom Christ had promised to his Church.

That certainly is correct. Yet the natural explanations for what happened undoubtedly interacted with the movements of the Spirit and had their own importance in producing the final result.

Dr. Stark comes up with some conclusions that challenge the conventional wisdom on why and how the Roman Empire converted to Christianity.

For one thing, contrary to what many people believe, Christianity was not a movement of the dispossessed—a haven for slaves and impoverished outcasts. Rather, it was based in the middle and upper classes, the solid citizens of the Empire.

In no way does this diminish the Church's preferential option for the poor. Still, the obvious fact is that the new religion grew much more rapidly among middle- and upper-class residents of the cities than it did in outlying areas where poor peasants lived.

Christianity's urban character in turn made it possible for the Christians to create an effective social welfare network for the relief of the elderly, widows, and orphans; for the establishment of Christian cemeteries; and for the creation and maintenance of places of worship, which were located at first in private homes.

Christianity also appealed to women because it treated them with a degree of respect and dignity they did not receive in paganism. "Within the Christian subculture," Stark writes, "women enjoyed a far higher status than did women in the Greco-Roman world at large."

Christianity, after all, recognized women as equal to men, children of God with the same supernatural destiny. And the Christian moral code, with its prohibition of polygamy, infidelity, divorce, birth control, abortion, infanticide, and other practices inimical to the best interests of women, changed their status from that of powerless serfs in bondage to men, to persons with dignity and rights—in the Church and in society.

Strange to say, epidemics also played a role. That was the case with an outbreak of disease that struck in A.D. 165 in the reign of Marcus Aurelius and in just fifteen years carried away up to a third of the empire's population—including the emperor himself—and also with another epidemic (probably measles) that hit in A.D. 251 and produced similarly horrendous demographic results.

These disasters favored the rise of Christianity, Stark contends, for three reasons: first, Christianity offered a more satisfying account, grounded in the doctrine of the Cross, of the redemptive meaning of suffering and death; second, the living out of "Christian values of love and charity" meant that when disasters struck, the Christians were better able to cope with them—and to survive; third, the loosening of social structures that accompanied and followed the epidemics contributed to the removal of social obstacles that had stood in the way of conversion.

In sum, Stark maintains, it was how Christians lived and how they treated other people that made the big difference. "To cities filled with homeless and the impoverished, Christianity offered charity as well as hope. To cities filled with newcomers and strangers, Christianity offered an immediate basis for attachments. To cities filled with orphans and widows, Christianity provided a new and expanded sense of family. To cities torn by violent ethnic strife, Christianity offered a new basis for social solidarity. And to cities faced with epidemics, fires, and earthquakes, Christianity offered effective nursing services."

A Christian apologist writing around the year A.D. 200 saw the situation much the same way. In the famous *Epistle to Diognetus* we read that the Christians were "not distinguished from the rest of mankind by either country, speech, or customs". Yet they were significantly different all the same.

"The whole tenor of their way of living stamps it as worthy of admiration and admittedly extraordinary. . . . They marry like all others and beget children; but they do not expose their offspring. Their board they spread for all, but not their bed. They find themselves in the flesh, but do not live according to the flesh. They spend their days on earth but hold citizenship in heaven. They obey the established laws, but in their private lives they rise above the laws. . . .

"In a word: what the soul is in the body, that the Christians are in the world."

Is there a lesson in that for us?

II

Popping the Question . . . of Faith

All of us come into contact with potential converts all the time, from family members and close friends to casual acquaintances. Frequently ask yourself, "Could *this* person be open to the faith?"

If the answer is yes, it may be that the next step is the simple, direct approach: ask. You may have to practice it in front of a mirror a few times, but eventually you'll be able to say, "Have you ever thought of becoming a Catholic?"

Yes, some people will be taken aback, and nearly all will be surprised. But in my experience, some also will be pleased, even flattered. The process has begun.

Don't imagine that I'm talking about approaching perfect strangers. Quite the contrary. If you aren't on the way to developing a genuine friendship with this potential new Catholic, the question will sound impertinent and insincere. If you are, though, you could be in for a surprise. Sometimes the answer may be, "I was waiting for someone to say that. Glad you asked." And sometimes you may hear your friend say the same thing many years later, after his entry into the Church caps something that began with your question.

"Of the many influences that led to my conversion," a man named Bob recalls, "three stand out: Chesterton, Newman, and the woman who would become my wife. The fundamental reason was an apprehension of truth. I came to think, with Chesterton, that Catholicism was the key that 'fits the lock, because it is like life'. I came to think, with Newman, that the historical case for Catholicism was irrefutable. And when the woman who would become my wife asked me the practical question, 'Well, are you going to convert or aren't you?' that was the last push I needed to place my bet."

To ask people to consider becoming Catholics means challenging them to consider making the most significant decision they will ever make in their lives, a decision vastly more important than the choice of school, profession, or even spouse. It's a decision that will affect the very fiber of their being in this life and have serious consequences in the life to come. If you can imagine yourself raising the question with others, you might do well first to read a book like William J. Whalen's *Separated Brethren* (Our Sunday Visitor), a survey of non-Catholic denominations that can help you understand where other people are coming from, religiously speaking.

Launching into the discussion of these matters with somebody means committing yourself to move far beyond the usual conversational trivia and go head to head with fundamental issues of meaning. Why are we here? What is truth? Are some things right and other things wrong? Is there a God? An afterlife? Is Jesus Christ God? Did he establish a church—and is it still around? If so, which one is it? Is it necessary to belong to the Catholic Church in order to be saved?

There is nothing new about all that, of course. In his encyclical *Fides et Ratio* (Faith and Reason), Pope John Paul points out that even a "cursory glance" at history shows people always have asked these things. And why shouldn't they? These are "questions which have their common source in the quest for meaning which has always compelled the human heart."

The quest for meaning still compels countless hearts today. It is our job—yours and mine—to help our friends in their search for the true answers.

Getting Up to Speed

Being an evangelist in today's world means being an apologist—someone who is able to answer people's questions about Catholicism and provide clear, reasonable explanations of why Catholics believe what they believe and do what they do.

Yes, I know, getting up to speed on all that is the work of a lifetime. To which my answer is: good—that's exactly how it should be. There's always more for any of us to learn about the faith (and that certainly includes me). But this is a case where learning on the job is definitely in order. Here's a consoling thought: no matter how little you may think you know, the friend you're talking with almost certainly knows even less.

Undoubtedly the most important part of it is knowing where to go for the answers we need. A lot of our catechetical work with potential converts will consist essentially of referring them to the best sources and probably consulting those sources ourselves.

Required Reading

Obviously, a good grasp of the New Testament and the Catechism of the Catholic Church is essential. Not that it's necessary to memorize either, but we need to be familiar with what they say, and we need to know where to go to look things up.

Stop and ask yourself: Do I have a pretty good idea of what's in the Letter to the Romans? Where do you find the Sermon on the Mount? If I need to know what the Catechism says about the infallibility of the Pope, how do I check on that? If you're in doubt about things like this, some brushing up is in order.

In addition, it's important slowly but systematically to read and study the great British and American apologists. I have in mind people like Newman, Chesterton, Benson, Knox, Lewis, Sheed, and Kreeft. And beyond what we read and study ourselves, we also need to be prepared to recommend good reading to people who express an interest in learning more about the faith.

I'll get back to the subject of reading and its great importance later; here let me say only that besides the apologetical works of the writers just mentioned, we will also want to point our friends to classic lives of Christ (Goodier, Sheen, Riccioti, Guardini) and reliable summaries of Catholic teaching (Trese, Hardon, Wuerl and Lawler) and encourage them to equip themselves with a good translation of the Bible that contains a helpful ascetical commentary (the Navarre Bible). The encyclicals and other writings of Pope John Paul II, including several of his books (e.g., *Crossing the Threshold of Hope*), also are important for understanding contemporary Catholic thought. But be aware that much of the Pope's writing is difficult and probably not for most beginners.

Very likely, too, at a certain point you will want to whet your friend's appetite with a book or books containing conversion stories: St. Augustine's *Confessions* and Cardinal Newman's *Apologia pro Vita Sua* are classics; Thomas Merton's *Seven Storey Mountain*, C. S. Lewis' *Surprised by Joy*, and Scott and Kimberly Hahn's *Rome, Sweet Home* are excellent examples of a more recent vintage; and *Spiritual Journeys* (Pauline Publications) is a fine collection by several hands. There are many other excellent works as well. It seems as if converts love to write about God's great favor in leading them to faith. One result of that is a bevy of good books.

Finally—and I'll say more about this later, too—encourage your friend to become familiar with the rich history of the Church, with all its ups and downs. Among other things, reading history makes clear the continuity of Catholicism, continuity stretching back to Christ and the Apostles, which deeply impresses many of those who enter the Church.

"That is what led me ineluctably to Rome," a young woman remarks, "for despite the importuning of well-meaning Evangelicals and Baptists, I could not see—and I still cannot see—any other true line from Christ himself through two thousand years to the present day except the line of souls that leads from him to St. Peter to . . . me." As an introduction to this marvelous story, I recommend Philip Hughes' one-volume *Popular History of the Church* (unfortunately out of print, but worth looking for) and Warren Carroll's multivolume *History of Christendom* (Christendom College Press).

Liturgy and Heart

Another important avenue for introducing our friends to the faith lies in exposing them to the spirituality and beauty of the Catholic liturgy (where it is beautifully celebrated, in beautiful surroundings, of course) and to art, literature, and music of Catholic inspiration.

It can give an impressive introduction to the incarnational, sacramental character of Catholicism to accompany someone to Mass, solemn benediction, a baptism, a wedding, the Easter Vigil, or the ordination of a bishop or of new priests. If you do that, though, be sure to prepare your friend for the experience in advance and to invite—and answer—his questions afterward.

Gregorian chant and great classical compositions centered on the Mass, the psalms, and events in the lives of our Lord and our Lady can draw people closer to belief. Mozart and Beethoven, Bruckner and Messiaen, Poulenc (*Dialogues of the Carmelites*) and other musical masters as evangelizers? Indeed yes!

Introduce your friends, too, to the great Catholic authors. There are so many—and the body of literature they've produced is so rich!—From Dante to Manzoni and Sienkiewicz, to Undset, Waugh, O'Connor (Flannery and Edwin both), Bernanos, Mauriac, and so many others. In reading them, people may very well glimpse the truth of something that Flannery O'Connor said:

> I don't think of conversion as being once and for all and that's that. I think once the process is begun and continues that you are continually turning inward toward God and away from your own egocentricity and that you have to see this selfish side of yourself in order to turn away from it. I measure God by everything that I am not.

But let's be realistic. Not everyone will be receptive to a highly intellectual or culturally oriented approach to Catholicism. For lots of people, much simpler materials—pamphlets rather than books, hymns rather than symphonies, the stained glass of a suburban church rather than Chartres—may be in order. Time spent praying with them or visiting the sick or making a pilgrimage to a local Marian shrine, Rosaries in hand, may count for more than reading encyclicals or the collected works of Thomas Aquinas. That just points again to the importance of *friendship*—of knowing people well and reaching out to them where they are.

Don't forget the parish and the priest. If your friend does become a Catholic, he almost certainly will spend the rest of his life worshipping in the setting of a Catholic parish. Here and now, moreover, actual entry into the Catholic Church these days is likely to be preceded by the candidate's participation in a parish-based RCIA (Rite of Christian Initiation of Adults) program extending over some months. So try to establish a team approach if you can, by directing your potentially Catholic friend to a prayerful, zealous priest who will join you in helping that person along the way.

And If the Answer Is No ...

But suppose that after a reasonable amount of time and effort, your friend just doesn't react, doesn't get it. He tells you he's given it a good shot, but he simply doesn't see the point. He has too many difficulties with Christ or Mary or the infallibility of the Pope or the Church or the Inquisition or something else. Maybe his spouse or his parents are insuperably opposed, and he doesn't want to hurt them.

What do you do then? Drop your friend cold and start looking for another prospective catch? Certainly not. Prayer, persistence, and patience come next. And constancy in friendship. The evidence that your love for your friend is for real may finally win him over. Bear in mind that you may be the one person in his life who is genuinely and disinterestedly concerned about his salvation. If he also comes to grasp that fact by the way you behave toward him, it can make a tremendous difference. Conversions happen according to God's timetable, not ours. *This* one may happen on a deathbed, with you watching from heaven.

But suppose your friend makes it—he's a Catholic. What now? If you've gotten a taste for "making" converts, you'll already have other friends in mind; indeed, you may be working with them already. At the same time, though, don't forget your new-Catholic friend. In religious and spiritual terms, he's a very young child, just taking his first steps in an unfamiliar setting where he has some surprises and some tumbles in store. He may be taking flak from others who regard his conversion as, in Chesterton's words, "a nuisance and a new and dangerous thing". In short, he needs your nurturing, your encouragement, your friendship and support.

"Sanctification is the work of a lifetime", St. Josemaria Escriva remarks. You have to be prepared to stick with your friend every step of the way. Entering the Church is one thing; being a spiritually vibrant member of the Body of Christ, with an active prayer life, frequent participation in the eucharistic sacrifice, fruitful and regular reception of the sacrament of penance, and all the rest—including an active apostolate of his own—is a joyous task that never ends this side of the grave.

You can't do it for your friend, but you can explain what is involved and provide continuing encouragement. The poet and convert Paul Claudel put it simply: "Tell him his only duty is to be joyful."

III

Opportunities and Obstacles

Why do people decide to become Catholics? And what sometimes keeps them from taking that step? The story of a woman I'll call Frieda suggests some answers to both questions.

"I came into full communion with the Roman Catholic Church at the Easter Vigil in 1997. I was forty-five. I'd been raised in the Congregational Church—later, the United Church of Christ—which is one of the most watered-down, liberal strains of Protestantism.

"I grew up in a very Protestant part of the Midwest, a Minneapolis suburb. The Catholics lived in St. Paul, which everyone considered inferior. My father was a Lutheran, and from him and my paternal grandparents I always heard the worst about Catholics. They were people who went to Mass on Saturday night and then went out and got drunk.

"In our town, Catholic children didn't transfer into public school until ninth grade. Until I reached ninth grade, I'd never met a Catholic. It wasn't until high school, really, that I got to know some Catholic girls. Even in the late sixties, their reputation for morality wasn't good. I became friends with two of them. One got pregnant in the eleventh grade, and the other came from a big family—seven or eight children—which was unheard of in Protestant circles. (There were four children in my family, and that was considered very many.)

"My experiences at our church were generally positive, mainly because of friends and a feeling of close-knit community. But then they fired the minister, who was a dear family friend, and did it in a very ugly, public way. The formation in Christian faith was bare bones. Our family went to church every Sunday and celebrated Christian holidays, but there was very little spiritual content to what we did. Our version of Christianity was largely focused on the virtues of honesty, hard work, charity, loyalty, etc. There wasn't much prayer.

"With this meager foundation, and with the bad taste from the minister's firing still in my mouth, I didn't go to church in college or for years afterward. Only when I experienced a personal crisis did I start looking for answers.

"I spent many years seeking them in a quasi-Christian but mostly New Age church called Unity. It had headquarters in Missouri. I felt I was finding some answers and experiencing some spiritual connection with God, but I also knew Unity wasn't the complete answer.

"Several Protestant friends attempted to steer me back to a mainline Protestant church. My husband and I tried several, since our three children were at an age to start receiving religious instruction. He was a fallen-away cradle Catholic who didn't much care about going to a Protestant church. He had grown up in a mixed-marriage family—father Catholic, mother Protestant—and that was a source of great tension in his childhood. So he was glad to go along now for the sake of family unity.

"As we visited one Protestant church after another, though, the desire to return to the Catholic Church awakened in him. He began going to Mass again with our oldest son.

"In the meantime my family of origin was in crisis. My parents had recently divorced. My mother suffered a stroke. One of my brothers committed suicide. And my father had a ruptured aorta that should have killed him but didn't.

"I was overwhelmed by all this suffering. My search took on a new urgency. Unity and the New Age offer you nothing on the subject of suffering, and I knew Protestantism didn't have a lot to say either. The best our culture could come up with was a popular book about why bad things happen to good people—and it was written by a rabbi.

"In the early nineties I was invited to give some talks to Opus Dei groups. I was struck by the kindness, warmth, depth, and piety of the people I met. I was surprised that Catholics could be like that. I began to think that the Catholic Church might have something to say to me about suffering. A good friend of mine invited me to go on a retreat and gave me many beautiful books to read. It looked like I was finally on the right path.

"I also started thinking about my husband's desire that the family all practice one religion in order to avoid the problems he'd experienced as a child. One day in the middle of 1996 I decided I wanted to become a Catholic. My husband was totally surprised and overjoyed.

"We had our children baptized that summer—they'd been 'baptized' with rose petals at Unity. I began RCIA classes that fall. In the spring of 1997 I received my First Communion! Only later did I learn how many people, including you, had been praying for my conversion."

How is Frieda's story typical? Searching for meaning and not finding it in other religious groups, anti-Catholic bigotry in the surrounding environment, experience of the mystery of evil and suffering—these things turn up over and over again in the accounts of people who finally come to the Catholic Church.

Probably you know some people like this, people at various stages of their journeys. If you care about them, the biggest favor you can possibly do them is give them a hand on the way.

Evangelizing in America: Historical Overview

This isn't the place to spend a great deal of time on either theory or history, but a quick once-over-lightly covering some of the religious and cultural background of Catholicism in the United States may help clarify where the Church in this country now finds herself and shed some light on the "big picture" challenges and opportunities we face where evangelization and conversion are concerned.

"Dogmas make nations", the French philosopher Joseph DeMaistre said. From the start, the overriding dogma of our country has been the absolute right of each individual to "life, liberty, and the pursuit of happiness" according to his own tastes.

That is emphatically true now. I fully expect that one of these days we will witness a serious campaign to make "go for it" the national motto. The saving message of Christ as it is mediated through his Church doesn't easily penetrate this individualistic, get-it-while-you-can mindset.

But that doesn't mean America hasn't been and isn't now a religious country. On the contrary, up to this time America has experienced several major waves of Christianization. Even now, from one point of view, it continues to be one of the most "religious" countries in the world.

The first stage in the evangelization of what is now the United States was the Spanish evangelization of Florida, Texas, and California starting in the late fifteenth century and continuing for several centuries after that. Next came the Christianization carried out by arrivals from northern Europe, notably the British and the French.

A few hundred years down the line, that was followed by the infusion of a distinct Catholic presence into areas up until then largely untouched by Catholicism. I mean the massive immigration of European Catholics—Irish, Germans,

Italians, Poles, and others—in the nineteenth and early twentieth centuries. Now something similar may be under way as a result of the huge influx of Hispanic immigrants from Mexico, Central America, and the Caribbean, and Catholics from the Philippines, Vietnam, and Korea.

In the early years of the nation, not only was the country as a whole sparsely populated, but the Catholic population in particular numbered only a tiny handful. In 1776, the year of American independence, all thirteen colonies had only twenty-four priests serving a flock of fewer than twenty-five thousand.

Scholars argue about how congenial the United States was to Catholicism in its first two centuries. On the level of theory, some hold that the foundational ideas of American democracy can be traced back to Scholastic, even Thomistic, thought; but others maintain that the fundamental assumptions and principles of our liberal democracy are grounded in the rationalism and individualism that were among the fruits of the anti-Christian Enlightenment of the eighteenth century.

Whichever side you take in that particular argument, it's an indisputable fact that, alongside the friendly surroundings offered to the Catholic Church by America's constitutionally enshrined religious toleration, an ugly undercurrent of anti-Catholicism has been present throughout and sometimes risen to the surface of American social life. At times this hostility has taken such truly despicable forms as convent burning, the lurid fantasies of Maria Monk, the Know-Nothing Movement, the American Protective Association, the KKK, and the bigotry that greeted Al Smith's campaign for president in 1928. More often, it has been a pervasive, unspoken fact of life. Much of American Catholic history, including the defensive tendency to be more American than the Americans, needs to be understood against this background of persistent tension and (at best) lightly veiled religious persecution.

The Inculturation of American Catholics

Has the problem of anti-Catholicism now been solved? In one sense it has. The solution has taken place through the thoroughgoing inculturation of American Catholics, which has occurred especially since World War II.

As a result of this process, the institutional and behavioral distinctiveness of Catholics that at one time set them apart from everybody else—fish on Friday, Saturday night confession, Sunday morning Mass, a social life organized around ethnic neighborhoods and ethnic parishes—has by now largely disappeared. Many if not most American Catholics are now just like everybody else, both for good and also for bad.

The mixed history of the Church in the United States also is reflected in the comparatively weak influence that Catholicism has had on American secular culture—weak, that is, in relation to Catholic numbers.

In earlier times the Church grew, to be sure, steadily and even dramatically, due to immigration and high birth rates. But it sometimes seemed as if spirituality and the intellectual life were given substantially less emphasis than the continual expansion of an institutional superstructure of churches, schools, and hospitals to serve a burgeoning Catholic population. Perhaps this was inevitable, but it had a price.

Although people sometimes claimed that the "Americanism" that Pope Leo XIII condemned in 1899 (in a letter called *Testem Benevolentiae* that was formally addressed to Cardinal Gibbons of Baltimore) was only a "phantom heresy", the emphasis placed by American Catholicism upon external activity and good works over the cultivation of the interior life was—and remains—a fact.

Moreover, it's hard to avoid the impression that the fairly simple-minded mistakes of Americanism provided a kind of bridge leading to the more complex and subtle errors of Modernism. This was the heresy that troubled the Church in France and other European countries early in the twentieth century and provoked a crisis in Catholicism that, nearly a century later, has still not been completely resolved.

Reinforcing the less-than-healthy tendencies in American Catholicism was a clericalism typical of (though by no means peculiar to) Irish Catholicism. Catholic lay people were exhorted and taught to be totally loyal to the Church and her clerical leaders; innovation and initiative in evangelizing the surrounding culture did not receive a high priority in this vision of Catholic life and the role of the laity.

And yet ... by all numerical measures, the Catholic Church in the United States grew by leaps and bounds.

By the middle years of the twentieth century, perceptive observers were aware that the American Catholic community was on its way to assuming not just prominence but cultural and religious preeminence.

In 1944 and 1945, for instance, the influential Protestant magazine *The Christian Century* published a series of articles with the title "Can Catholicism Win America?" For editor Harold Fey, the answer was obvious: yes.

The rise of Catholicism continued for another two decades, into the mid-1960s. Catholic families typically had numerous children. The rate of Sunday Mass attendance was around 75 percent (that is to say, on any given Sunday morning, about three Catholics out of four were in church). Catholics regularly and frequently went to confession. Catholic elementary and secondary schools enrolled five million students. Seminaries and religious houses were full. American

Catholic missionaries served in mission lands all over the world. As many saw it, the great symbol that the Catholic Church had "arrived" was the election of the first Catholic president of the United States, John F. Kennedy.

American Catholicism Today

And now?

American Catholicism at the midpoint of the first decade of the twenty-first century is in some ways disturbingly reminiscent of western European Catholicism as it was two or three decades ago. The inroads of pernicious secularization are already highly visible and rapidly getting worse. The word *crisis* may have been overworked in describing the current situation of the Church in the United States, but, whether the word is overworked or not, the crisis is real.

The level of theological discourse in American Catholicism has traditionally been somewhat shallow—not surprising, considering the immigrant character of the Church during much of this time. In the last three decades or so, however, theological thinking—as well as seminary training, the teaching of theology in colleges and universities, and catechetics—has been largely under the sway of dissident theology reflecting the influence of secular figures like Marx, Hegel, Freud, and Kant.

These years have witnessed the faddish popularity of such theological schools as liberation theology; process theology; "transcendental Thomism"; and, in morals, consequentialism and proportionalism. The practical results, occurring through a trickle-down process of miseducation and malformation, have been disastrous for the faith and morals of American Catholics as a group.

A great deal has been said and written about these matters. The aim here isn't to add to that existing body of literature. Here instead are just a few high points (or low points, if you prefer) that will help round out this scene setting.

—At the same time that some in the Church have failed to teach clearly and provide firm, forward-looking leadership, others have failed to listen obediently to what was taught (by the Pope and by solid orthodox bishops and others) and to follow the directives they received. Opinion polls show sharp declines in Catholics' respect for episcopal authority in the wake of revelations about clergy sex abuse and its cover-up by some bishops.

—Not at all coincidentally, these tendencies have combined with a serious falling off in the quality and even the quantity of catechesis. As a result, we now have one-going-on-two generations of Catholics who have been given little or no formal religious education or else only dimly remember what they may once have received. Things have reached the point where something the Archbishop of Salzburg in Catholic Bavaria said three centuries ago fits many otherwise well-educated American Catholics today: "The common man cannot even say the Lord's Prayer or the Ave Maria and does not know the Apostles' Creed, to say nothing of the Ten Commandments."

—Against this background, it's hardly surprising that various indices of Catholic religious practice and commitment look as bad as they do. The rate of Sunday Mass attendance in the United States is now around one in three—and far lower than that in some places. The number of priests fell from 59,000 in 1965 to 46,000 in 2002, the number of seminarians from 49,000 to 4,700, the number of religious sisters from 180,000 to 75,500. Many of the priests and sisters are in their seventies, and the median age is rising fast. The percentage of parishes without resident priests rose from 3 percent in 1965 to 15 percent in 2002. A growing number of church and school closings adds to the impression of widespread institutional collapse.

—The state of Catholic attitudes also is profoundly disturbing. One poll, whose results are typical of many others, traced opinion shifts between 1987 and 1999 on whether it was possible to be a "good Catholic" in various circumstances: without obeying Church teaching on abortion—39 percent yes in 1987, 53 percent yes in 1999; without giving time and money to the poor—44 percent in 1987, 56 percent in 1999. Questions about not attending Sunday Mass, practicing birth control, divorcing and remarrying, and marrying outside the Church produced similar results. As of 1999, 38 percent of Catholics thought it was possible to be a good Catholic without believing in Christ's Real Presence in the Blessed Sacrament, while 23 percent thought the same about believing in Jesus' physical Resurrection from the dead.

Faced with numbers like these, the temptation is strong to throw up your hands in despair. That would be a terrible mistake.

For one thing, even though there are many uninstructed, nonpracticing, indifferent Catholics in the United States, there also are many who are firm in their faith and ardent in living it out. One result of the crisis has been the emergence of a corps of truly exemplary Catholics—many of them lay people, along with many priests and religious—whose response to hard times is to try harder themselves.

Serving them, too, are many new institutions—schools, publishing houses, periodicals, media—committed to orthodoxy and evangelization. New bishops have appeared on the scene ready and determined to preach the gospel fearlessly; zealous young priests are being ordained. New Catholic groups and movements are springing up on all sides. The enormous success in 2004—in the face of vicious opposition from the cultural elites—of Mel Gibson's powerful film *The Passion of the Christ* showed that millions of Americans are eager to hear the gospel message and get to know Jesus.

These people and these institutions and programs are the strong nucleus of the new evangelization that is coming in America. It's about that which we'll speak next.

IV

The Impulse to Convert

The crisis in American Catholicism hasn't come about in a vacuum. The last forty years have brought a wide-ranging cultural crisis—a crisis of faith and morality, really—in the United States as well as in other Western countries, where secularization has gone even further and deeper. The crisis in the United States and in the Church here can be seen, in part at least, as one aspect of this larger crisis.

In our nation as in others, over these decades a process of moral decline set in and became institutionalized. Decadence acquired a constituency. The United States is in far worse shape as a result of what has happened, even though the people in universities and media and big secular foundations and courts and legislatures who did such a lot to produce this result are hardly about to admit it. On the contrary, these folks are much more likely to blame the "religious right" for the nation's problems.

The Escape from Decadence

But there is more to the story than this, and it's good news. For a growing number of Americans it's precisely the pervasive and perverse presence of moral decadence in the surrounding secular culture that led them to Catholicism. "What initially attracted me to the Church", one man writes from

Moscow, where he has worked for several years and lives with his wife and four children, "was her unequivocal position in defense of the unborn. This then led to a general moral awakening and then a spiritual one."

"I was attracted to the faith", reports another, a young man named Jack, "because the Catholic Church offered a clear and compelling defense of human life and because she also offered the only sane approach to human sexuality.

"As someone who witnessed, and to some extent experienced, the spiritual, emotional, and physical wreckage associated with the sexual revolution at my university, I was looking for a church whose teachings could help me make sense of the pain this 'revolution' caused. My own Episcopal Church could not. In fact, I was surprised and disappointed to learn that the male and female student leaders of my local Episcopal student group were living together.

"Experiences like this helped push me to look at my ecclesial options. Rome became ever more attractive, the more I learned about her moral teachings."

Bob reached the same conclusion by a somewhat different route. An Episcopalian by baptism, an atheist in college, and an Evangelical Protestant later in life, he'd begun to feel an attraction to Catholicism. Then a "personal model"—Pope John Paul II—pushed him to the very brink of conversion.

It was 1994. The United Nations was having one of its periodic world population conferences, this time in Cairo. The administration of President Bill Clinton and the governments of most nations in the wealthy, developed West were aggressively pushing a coercive proabortion, pro-population-control line. Standing against them was John Paul II.

For his pains, the Pope became the target of withering criticism aimed at him by the elite secular media in the United States. Many American Catholics became nervous and embarrassed in the face of this secularist barrage and started making apologies for the Pope's courageous stand. What was happening in Cairo also caught Bob's attention—and he definitely liked what he saw. As he recalls it, "The U.S. delegation tried to force unlimited abortion—an attempt to impose controversial policy and questionable morality on the entire world.

"A lone voice in the wilderness, Pope John Paul spoke out. Soon Muslim clerics fell in behind him [as did, it might be added, some Latin American governments]. John Paul's moral leadership saved the day.

"I was deeply impressed by the Church's capacity through her leader to mobilize for good. By now, I was barely a Protestant."

And soon, predictably, he became a Catholic.

For Jennie, too, the abortion issue was what made the difference.

"I walked away from religion in high school," she writes, "but later found my will to oppose God crumbling in college. A huge wall collapsed the day I saw *The Silent Scream*, a movie about the pain babies feel during abortions. It had been produced by the ex-abortionist—and now Catholic—Dr. Bernard Nathanson.

"I left the movie in tears. I said I resented this 'right-wing propaganda'—but, for the first time in a long while, I knew that truth existed and I had a chance to seek it again.

"A 'woman's right to abortion' had been an article of faith in my individualistic life. By an act of the will, I'd made my own opinions the framework for my understanding of the world. *The Silent Scream* forced me to face the fact that there were limits to autonomy. It was one thing for me, tipsy over dinner, to declare to my college friends that although abortion was murder, freedom does have its costs. It was something quite different to be forced to face the fact that the cost of that particular freedom was the scream of a helpless, dying child."

Sometime later Jennie moved to Washington. One day she came to see me.

"What brings you to sit in my office?" I asked.

"I am looking for the truth about Jesus Christ and about the Catholic Church", she said.

"Oh. You're a goner."

And so she was.

When the Bottom Falls Out

As with Frieda, quoted above, so also in other cases it is the personal experience of suffering and collapse that brings people face to face with God and the claims of the Church. Success comes easy and in a big way for some people in our affluent, celebrity-conscious culture. But so do defeat and disaster. And what do you do then, when the bottom falls out in a way for which nothing up to that time has prepared you?

That was the question that faced economic and financial guru Lawrence Kudlow. For some time, due to the efforts of friends, he'd been looking into Catholicism and had been talking to me. For an even longer time, however, he'd battled alcohol and cocaine addiction. "In the spring of 1995," he told an interviewer from *Crisis* magazine, "the roof fell down on my life.

"I had another bad relapse. I lost my jobs and my life in the spring of 1995. My wife sent me away to the Hazelden Treatment Center in Minnesota. I was there for five months."

There things turned around for him. He sobered up. He attended Sunday Mass. He did some serious reading. He kept in touch with me and his Catholic friends. When he left the treatment center he found work, reunited with his wife, and kept on moving toward the Church. On November 20, 1997, he was baptized in Manhattan, surrounded by Catholic friends from what he calls "the *National Review* gang".

"All of this is God's handiwork", Larry Kudlow says. "I have learned to live a life of faith. . . . I pray and meditate every single day, every morning. You know, I pray in cabs. I pray in airplanes. I don't really ask for anything—I just pray that Jesus will give me the strength to follow him. That's all I pray for. And that I will always turn my will and my life over to his care."

The Importance of Fidelity

Many converts also attest to the importance of the doctrinal fidelity—the adherence to the Christian tradition—that they find in the Catholic Church. During a Vatican meeting, the distinguished American novelist Walker Percy, himself a convert, put the importance of fidelity like this in speaking of "one aspect of the matter of the evangelization of culture" that he feared cradle Catholics might overlook: "It is, or was for me, the very steadfastness of the Church, which is perhaps its most noticeable mark, a steadfastness which is, of course, a scandal and a contradiction to some and a sign to others, as grace permits. . . .

"By remaining faithful to its original commission, by serving its people with love, especially the poor, the lonely, and the dispossessed, and by not surrendering its doctrinal steadfastness, sometimes the very contradiction of culture by which it serves as a sign, surely the Church serves the culture best."

A friend of mine named Morgan, having made many other stops on the way before he reached Catholicism, puts it more concretely: "I came to the Church by the most roundabout route. As a Protestant, I thought of the world as two groups of Christians, Protestants and Catholics. I was a Protestant. I could no more become a Catholic than I, a white man, could become a woman or black. I might become a Buddhist or a Confucian, but not a Catholic.

"So it was a great surprise when I found myself before the doors of the Church of Rome. But God knew better than I. If I had been led to those doors immediately after my reconversion to Christianity, I would not have gone in. It was necessary for me to explore many other Christian possibilities, circling around, ever closer, until it was the Church of Rome I spotted through the forest.

"I was not interested in any brand of Christianity that was not faithful to the most 'unbelievable' fact in history—that Jesus Christ, the Son of God, was crucified unto death in order to redeem us (me!) from sin. There is not, nor has there ever been, anything I am surer of than that. And only the Catholic Church seemed willing to cling to it.

"So then I was ready to come in. God had prepared me. By that time I just wanted to live where God was, and I knew he was in the tabernacle behind the altar."

Whose Job Is It?

For centuries, Catholic lay people have for the most part tended to be hesitant to accept their responsibility for "making" converts. That isn't true of all, of course—some of the laity have been zealous firebrands of the faith. But many have been pretty much content to leave this particular job more or less exclusively in the hands of the clergy. If someone became a Catholic, that naturally was a good thing. But offering active encouragement to others to take this step was, as they saw it, no business of theirs.

That attitude was and is a terrible mistake, an abdication of a duty that comes with baptism and membership in the Church. Approximately 98.5 percent of the Catholics in the world are laypersons. Leaving it entirely up to the other 1.5 percent to proclaim the gospel and lead people to Christ just doesn't make sense.

On the contrary, as people mature in their knowledge and practice of the faith, they should naturally shoulder more and more responsibility for reaching out to family members, colleagues at work, neighbors, and friends and seeking to share the faith with them. Feelings of inadequacy regarding one's knowledge—or lack of knowledge—of the Church are no excuse. As I remarked earlier, virtually any Catholic at least knows more about Catholicism than his non-Catholic friends do. And if there are serious gaps in that knowledge, that only underlines the need—which exists in any case—to go about systematically filling them through personal study and consulting others.

What's so strange, I ask you, about the idea of trying to lead people to the faith? People aren't shy about recommending restaurants, movies, TV shows, and a great deal else of very minor importance to those they care about. Are Jesus Christ and his Church of less importance than the greatest new sushi place in town or the hottest new flick of the last six months?

Certainly the clergy have a role to play in this process. But it's not that of sitting in a rectory office and issuing orders to the laity—or, much less, doing all the work themselves. Preaching the gospel in deed and in word comes with being a Christian. When Jesus said, "Go therefore and make disciples of all nations" (Mt 28:19), he wasn't talking only to the Apostles—he meant each of us.

When it comes to bringing people to the faith, the priest's role is essentially twofold: first, forming and educating the laity for their apostolic mission on the front lines, out there in the world; and second, being the deal closers, if you will, who counsel and instruct prospective converts and take the necessary sacramental steps—baptism, penance, confirmation, Eucharist—that carry them definitively into the Church.

A Sermon for Our Times

I have a dream that one of these days a conscientious new pastor is going to get up in the pulpit of his church and say something like this:

"My dear brothers and sisters in Christ:

"I want you to understand that my associates and I are here above all to preach, to administer the sacraments, and to catechize. We do these things for you, our parishioners, so that you can do a better job of bringing Christ—and *being* Christ—to your families and your neighborhoods, to the people where you work and go to school, to your community, your nation, your culture, your world.

"That being the case, I'm here to tell you not to worry about it if you don't have time to get so heavily involved doing things in the parish—lay ministries, committees, all that. Those things are good, and we priests welcome the participation of those among you who are able to lend a hand in that way. But doing things in the parish isn't your first and most important job as Catholic lay people.

"Your job is to go out and change the world—to do what it takes to place Christ at the summit of all human activity and to help more and more people know him and accept him and love and serve him.

"That's what it's all about. Please let us priests know how we can help you laity do it better."

Stephen's Story

Finally, to round out the discussion of obstacles and opportunities, let me share with you the story of a friend of mine whom I'll call Stephen. In its own way, it sums up a lot of what's been said.

"I grew up in a 'mixed marriage' between a Presbyterian and an Episcopalian. But because we lived much of the time abroad, in Latin America, we pretty much had to take whatever English-speaking Protestant church was available. As a result, my religious upbringing could best be described simply as mainstream Protestant. When I was a young teenager, nevertheless, my religious interests were active enough that I requested confirmation in the Presbyterian Church (which doesn't perceive confirmation as sacramental, of course).

"By the time I got to Princeton, I was heavily involved in the conservative political scene. But I was essentially a libertarian and had largely rejected serious religion, which I took to be simply a helpful force in preserving social and political order.

"Even so, after I had spent a mainly decadent freshman year, religious interests started to stir in my soul again when I was a sophomore. I began to attend the ultraliberal Presbyterian church near the campus and then the Episcopalian church. But I wasn't satisfied. Odd as it may seem, the preaching sounded unbiblical to me.

"That is when an old interest in the mystique of Catholicism reemerged. Growing up in Latin America, I'd been surrounded by the trappings of Catholicism, had many Catholic friends, and had always had great respect for the Catholic faith. I knew very little about it. All I really knew was that when Hollywood wants to depict the paradigm of a religious figure, it isn't a Presbyterian minister—it's a Catholic priest. When someone needs to be exorcised, they don't call in Pastor Joe, they call in Father Jones.

"When I spoke about what I was feeling, a good friend, whom I knew to be a devout Catholic, expressed pleasure at what I said. The next Sunday we went to Mass together. Soon I started to ask questions and receive instruction. The more I learned, the more I asked. The religious question became more and more important to me, and I realized that I was asking about the basics—the existence of God, the inspiration of the Bible, the role of the Church, and so on.

"That began a year-long process of discernment, during which I kept wrestling with my questions and read Church history. Eventually I concluded that Jesus Christ had established a Church during his lifetime on earth, that that Church still exists, and that only the Catholic Church can credibly claim lineage extending back to the time of Christ himself.

"I had difficulties, including, at first, Marian doctrines and moral issues like contraception and even abortion. But good reading—in Cardinal Newman, G. K. Chesterton, C. S. Lewis, and apologists like Peter Kreeft and Karl Keating—helped immensely. Talking to the parish priests finally pushed me over the edge. In the end, my conversion was largely intellectual.

"The following year, when I was getting ready to be confirmed at the Easter Vigil, I started coming by Mercer House now and then. The books you recommended and especially the life of prayer instilled by Louis in our chats proved to be immeasurably helpful. I doubt that otherwise my intellectual conversion would so easily have deepened into a conversion of the heart. Catholicism began to permeate my whole life. In a way, I had a 'second' conversion. I hope that makes sense."

Terrific sense. Oh, I nearly forgot—Stephen is now a Catholic priest.

V

Making Converts

"An Episcopalian by baptism, a 'liberated' atheist in college, reluctantly cognizant of Providence in the strivings and wanderings of my early career, I fancied myself well trained. I took pride in a healthy Enlightenment scepticism that sniggered at the alleged hypocrisies and superstitions of organized religion. I was a rationalist. Bertrand Russell was a hero."

So begins a banker's account of his conversion. What finally brought this confirmed sceptic to embrace the faith? He explains, "Doctrine. Universality. Authority. The Pope. The sacraments."

That's a pretty good list. And not unlike the one supplied by a book publisher telling what also drew him to the Church: "In my mind, the attractions of Catholicism were the consistency of its positions on things, its ability to take a stand on issues and to deal with internal problems, the vastness and worldwide nature of the institution—and the thought of a Mass taking place somewhere in the world every minute of every day. All these things helped convince me to proceed."

Lots of strong feeling ordinarily goes into the experience of conversion, and experience is an important part of living out our faith. Catholicism, after all, is a sacramental, tactile, sight-and-sound kind of religion whose founder had the foresight to set it up in such a way that it appeals to our senses and our emotions as well as to our intellects. But it is not, finally, the kind of feel-good religion that trades in emotion and not a whole lot else. At the core of Catholicism are matters of profound truth, pointing to one who is himself the Truth. It is essential not to lose sight of that.

In case there may ever have been any doubt, readers who've gotten this far will be fully aware by now that this isn't a technical, theological book. (I trust it's grounded in orthodox theology and sound practice, but that's a different question.) At this point nevertheless it may be helpful if we pause for a bit and take a closer look at a few terms. I hope this doesn't become overly dry. But it may help clarify some of the things that have already been said and shed light on some things that are yet to come.

Defining Our Terms

Start with *evangelization*—it comes from a Greek word that means good news. As for the "good news" itself, that's another name for the gospel—the message of redemption and the coming of the kingdom of God, which Jesus Christ proclaimed and then entrusted to his followers—"Go into all the world and preach the gospel to the whole creation" (Mk 16:15)—beginning with the Apostles and continuing all the way to us.

An *evangelist*, needless to say, is someone who does this work (the "four Evangelists" are the authors of the four Gospels, Matthew, Mark, Luke, and John, who did it in a special way). As for *evangelization*, it's the process of doing it.

Pope John Paul's splendid encyclical *Redemptoris missio* (*The Mission of the Redeemer*) begins with a dramatic, no-nonsense statement of the challenge that confronts us: "The mission of Christ the Redeemer, which is entrusted to the Church, is still very far from completion. As the second millennium after Christ's coming draws to an end [the encyclical is dated December 7, 1990], an overall view of the human race shows that this mission is still only beginning and that we must commit ourselves wholeheartedly to its service. It is the Spirit who impels us to proclaim the great works of God: 'For if I preach the gospel, that gives me no ground for boasting. For necessity is laid upon me. Woe to me if I do not preach the gospel!'" (1 Cor 9:16).

At first, this may sound pretty surprising. After two thousand years the work is "still only beginning"? We're tempted to ask how that can possibly be. But think about it, and you'll see it's true. Bear in mind that of the over six billion people in the world today, only a few over one billion are Catholics, and only another billion or so are members of other Christian denominations. That leaves some four billion people who, practically speaking, haven't heard the good news of Christ.

There are many means and instruments of evangelization, but, as has been emphasized repeatedly here, the most effective means of evangelizing today is—as it has always been—individual, personal apostolate, the apostolate of friendship. Other evangelizing instruments—the media, for example—can and should be used, but nothing will ever take the place of one friend speaking the good news to another.

Next, *conversion*. The Latin original signifies the act or experience of turning around. In a religious context, conversion fundamentally refers to turning away from sin and turning to God.

In that sense, every Catholic is, or should be, a convert—someone who has turned (or, as we might say in computer talk, has been "configured") to Christ and his Church. For cradle Catholics, this conversion is something that first occurs in baptism, when their parents—making this decision for them, as they make every other decision at that age—present them to be baptized. But it doesn't—or at least it shouldn't—end with that.

Turning more completely away from sin and turning ever more perfectly to God is a process that is meant to continue throughout life. Literally, it's one of those cradle-to-the-grave things. An adult Catholic who is growing in his faith, as all adult Catholics ought to be doing, is one who is experiencing the ongoing process of conversion that lies at the very heart of Christian life.

Within this general framework, conversion also has another, more particular, sense. It is the sense in which, most of the time, the word is being used in this book. That sense of conversion refers to the free act by which a person decides to move from some other church or religious denomination or belief system (or, often enough, some system of nonbelief) and become a member of ("fully in communion with") the Catholic Church, believing what the Church believes and seeking to live as the Church holds disciples of Jesus Christ ought to live.

Once this free commitment of faith has been made, of course, the new convert is immersed in the same process of ongoing conversion as every other Catholic. The ascetical life—that is, the life of ongoing struggle to grow in virtue and holiness—is the path of continuing conversion to Christ.

Here the saints are our models and guides. Virtually all of the saints were men and women who led lives of prayer and sacramental piety shaped by self-denial and penance. Through frequent examinations of conscience and sacramental confession, and with the help of prudent spiritual direction, they went on "converting" all during their lives. We need to learn from them.

Proselytism, Good and Bad

What about *proselytism*? It has a bad name these days. But here, I think, a distinction is in order.

Proselytism deserves to have a bad name if it means efforts to manipulate or coerce people into signing up with some belief system, whether it be a religion or anything else. In this sense, the Communists and the Nazis were in their day as guilty of proselytizing as any Christians ever were. And in our own times, the secular humanism that pervades the elite secular culture of the United States and other Western countries proselytizes energetically through the opinion-forming institutions it largely controls, including our universities and our media. But don't expect the secular humanists to admit that or even to recognize it. In most cases, they have been too thoroughly proselytized themselves to do that.

But proselytism also has an entirely benign sense. After all, members of any organization or group who believe in what it's doing quite naturally and benevolently want other people to become part of it. Haven't friends of yours ever said to you in so many words, "Join us in what we're doing—it's great"? If so, you know what I mean. It's like that with teams, clubs, political parties, and countless other groups where people come together for some form of personal fulfillment and service to others.

And it's like that with the Catholic Church. Any serious Catholic who considers the faith the most important thing in his life, that which colors and shapes and gives ultimate meaning and value to everything else, will naturally be motivated—and delighted—to share the faith with others.

For such a person, it will be a source of great joy if eventually he can be sponsor at a friend's entry into the Church (or return to the Church, in the case of a lapsed Catholic) or can help someone else discern God's call to a life of total dedication, whether as a priest, religious, or lay person. Obviously there can be no coercion or manipulation in these matters. It is imperative that such choices be authentically free. But there can be—and there should be—a generous, open-hearted invitation to spread the happiness that comes with being a follower of Christ in his true Church.

What does that happiness consist in? Many things, no doubt. But bear in mind something said earlier: Catholicism isn't a feel-good religion. For many people, the greatest joy in being or becoming a Catholic consists in having true answers to the perennial questions that Pope John Paul speaks of in his great encyclical *Fides et ratio* (*Faith and Reason*): "Who am I? Where have I come from and where am I going? Why is there evil? What is there after this life?" The genuine, definitive, life-affirming answers to these questions are found in Jesus Christ and his Church.

Apologetics. Apologetics doesn't mean making excuses. It means giving sound reasons and explanations for the faith, as the first letter of St. Peter explains: "Always be prepared to make a defense to any one who calls you to account for the hope that is in you, yet do it with gentleness and reverence" (1 Pet 3:15).

The Catholic Church has been blessed with many great apologists over the centuries. Before and during the Protestant Reformation, we have St. Thomas More and St. Peter Canisius. In the era of the Catholic Counter-Reformation, we have towering figures like St. Robert Bellarmine and St. Francis de Sales. Later centuries brought Cardinal Newman, G.K. Chesterton and Hilaire Belloc, Ronald Knox, C.S. Lewis, Archbishop Fulton Sheen—the list goes on and on.

The New Apologetics

In the decades since the Second Vatican Council, there has been a shift in apologetics away from simply defending the faith to spreading it. Without losing its grounding in sound arguments, apologetics has become more centered on Christ as he is present in Scripture. During the last two decades in the United States there has been a veritable explosion in this new apologetics, reflected in magazines, videos, Web sites, conferences, and the splendid ongoing work of the Eternal Word Television Network.

It is notable, too, that the new apologetics is largely the work of Catholic lay people, many of them converts to the Church and often from evangelical backgrounds. They have brought refreshing energy, humor, and learning to a field once dominated by dusty tracts. The good arguments are still there, but the emphasis is on joyful living of the fullness of truth found in Christ's Church.

The towering figures in this continuing renewal of Catholic apologetics include people like Karl Keating, Peter Kreeft, Scott Hahn, and many others. They have produced a rich cornucopia of print and audiovisual materials. Time and again I've found their work enormously helpful in guiding people to faith. Here are a few testimonials to that.

"Good reading in Cardinal Newman, G.K. Chesterton, C.S. Lewis, and apologists like Peter Kreeft and Karl Keating helped immensely."

"I came to think, with Chesterton, that Catholicism was the key that 'fits the lock, because it is like life'. I came to think, with Newman, that the historical case for Catholicism was irrefutable."

"I also read, from cover to cover, Guardini's *The Lord*."

"Our friend recommended twelve books, including several by Frank Sheed, Chesterton, and C. S. Lewis, and St. Teresa of Avila's *Life*."

"A few days before spring break, you handed me *Spiritual Journeys*, a book of conversion stories published by the Daughters of St. Paul. On Saturday evening I went to do my laundry and took the book with me to pass the time. After reading a half dozen of the stories, I saw a common thread: several evangelicals converted after abandoning their individual interpretation of Scripture and accepting divine revelation as interpreted by the Magisterium of the Church. A light bulb went on."

Now, *that's* what I call apologetics.

And, lastly, there is *catechesis*. This and other words like it (catechist, catechetics, catechism, catechumen, etc.) come from the Greek word for instruction. So catechesis is instruction in the faith, catechetics is the science of giving such instruction, a catechist is someone who gives it, a catechumen is someone who receives it, and so on.

As is well known, in the United States and many other countries there was a virtual collapse of catechesis during much of the period following Vatican Council II. "Experience" received priority in religious education, while substantive content was sharply downplayed. When content did get taught, not infrequently it was the "content" of heretical or heterodox views that placed the Church's dogmatic and moral teaching in doubt.

We are still paying for such mistakes today, with the payment taking the form of religious indifference on the part of many nominal Catholics who are fundamentally ignorant of their faith, along with the continued efforts of "progressives" to propagate their dissent. If I had to make a guess, I'd guess that perhaps one American Catholic out of ten could now be considered fully and correctly formed in the faith.

Help Is on the Way

But help is on the way. Thanks to the initiative of Pope John Paul II—an initiative opposed, incidentally, by many dissenting theologians and "progressive" stalwarts of the religious education establishment—we now have in hand a marvelous, comprehensive, up-to-date exposition of Catholic belief and practice called the Catechism of the Catholic Church. In time—and it can't possibly come too soon—all Catholic textbooks and other materials for religious education will be based on and faithfully reflect the contents of this splendid work.

Fortunately, too, in the last decade or so the American bishops have awakened to the problem posed by nonexistent or defective catechesis and to the opportunity for remedying the situation presented by the Catechism of the Catholic Church. Now they are taking serious steps to see that Catholic religious education texts teach what the Catholic Church teaches. That is a welcome move in the right direction.

All these things are relevant to the question of conversion, in several different ways.

For one thing, I've often encountered the phenomenon of the cradle Catholic or longtime convert who, practically speaking, fell away from the Church for lack of solid teaching.

In one such case—perhaps unwisely—I told a woman who came to see me about her failing marriage, brandishing a couple of degrees in religion from prestigious universities as she did, that she was an "ill-informed Catholic". Strangely enough, and thanks to the grace of God, she thought that statement over and then agreed that I was right.

"So began a period of spiritual growth", she recalls. "Being a Catholic was important to me, even if, as I eventually recognized, I hadn't understood, much less lived, its fundamentals." Now she does.

And then there is the phenomenon of the would-be convert who enters a parish RCIA program and gets less-than-positive results.

"[I was] taught by lay people with dubious credentials and little knowledge", reports a man named Don. And a man named Geoffrey, who badly wanted to become a Catholic, says he found RCIA "a total bore".

"I just did not connect," he recalls, "and in the first week of December I dropped out. One day at work, sitting at my desk, the thought came to me: 'It's over.' My journey into Catholicism was finished."

Fortunately, God had other plans, and now Geoffrey is happily Catholic. But it took some doing—some solid catechesis—to overcome the effects of a shallow RCIA program.

Don't misunderstand me—there also are excellent RCIA programs, and I could tell stories about those. But even the good programs have a tendency to drop people once they've gone through the Easter Vigil ceremonies and are considered to be safely "in". That is a bad mistake. For RCIA graduates—as for everyone else—continuing education in the faith is an absolute necessity. The new Catholic needs much nurturing, encouragement, and support in regard to the doctrinal dimension of the faith and in regard to living it out. This also is an important part of the "convert-making" apostolate.

When has someone studied enough? When does a person know all that one needs to know about Catholicism? The answer, of course, is never. Ongoing, systematic education and formation are essential. And although some people have the self-discipline and sophistication to take care of this on their own, most are well advised to find an orthodox formation program and spiritual director and turn to them as guides.

Finally, I'll offer a word of advice to those who may feel inclined to reach out to family members and friends, who would like to invite them to think of joining the Church but who feel they don't really know enough themselves to engage in serious religious conversation and answer serious questions and objections that may result.

This is the advice: learn. As I keep saying, you almost certainly know more about the Catholic Church than your family member or friend does. And what you don't know you can pick up as you go along—for your own sake as well as his—by reading and study.

The time to start is now. Get to work.

VI

Who Are the Converts?

Who are these prospective converts?

The first, and probably most important, answer is that they are people like you and me. In other words, men and women trying to make sense of life and find their way to heaven amid the temptations and confusions thrown in their paths by those well-known enemies, the world, the flesh, and the devil. The big difference is that most of us were lucky enough either to be born into the Catholic Church or to have already stumbled into it, whereas these folks are still scratching their heads and making up their minds.

Within that general framework, prospective converts fall into several distinct, identifiable groups. The people within these groups are important; they matter immeasurably, not as representatives of types and groups, but as individual human beings whom God has created and loved. But if the members of any one group have a certain priority that makes a demand on our attention and concern over and above all the rest, it's the lapsed and lukewarm Catholics who need to be brought back to the faith. (Instead of calling them converts, maybe we should start calling them "reverts".)

The Lapsed and the Lapsing

There are millions of these prodigal sons and daughters in today's United States. Indeed, it sometimes is said that

Catholics are the largest religious group in the country—and fallen-away Catholics the second largest. Moreover, a huge number are somewhere in between. They are in the process of falling away, as is apparent from the fact that only about one American Catholic in three now attends Mass regularly. That leaves forty-five million or so who attend Mass infrequently—the Christmas-and-Easter Catholics—or else never. Such people must be considered religiously at risk.

But why give priority to the lapsed and lapsing? The reason can be simply put: family feeling. These people are, or were, our brothers and sisters in the faith. If the Church is something like a family, these are family members who are seriously ill.

We should reach out to them with compassion, knowing that without prompt attention, they may die. We need to approach them as if we were emergency medical technicians of the faith, conscious that, just as many of our fallen-away family members and friends are probably only one good confession away from being reconciled with Christ, so also all of them are, like the rest of us, only one heartbeat away from giving God an accounting for how they've lived their lives.

Lydia's Story

Why do people drift away from the Church, and why do they come back? Lydia's story sheds light on that.

Lydia had been raised a Protestant, but she had entered the Church as a young woman. She'd been a Catholic—of sorts—for twenty-eight years at the time she came to see me about trouble in her marriage. Having heard her out, I recommended that she go to confession.

"Repentance is the beginning of true conversion of the heart", she writes. "It's step one of the Christian walk, the turn away from sin to God. When pride diminishes, charity can grow."

That is how it looks to her now. At the time, it wasn't so clear.

"I was twenty-eight years a Catholic. I didn't think I had any sins of serious concern. What was personal sin anyway? Sure, I had imperfections, I'd made mistakes, and, if provoked, I could be unkind. But like most other Americans, I was a pretty good person—indeed, I was better than most.

"Of course, in my present tragedy, I had no trouble identifying other peoples' outrageous offenses. I could talk about them endlessly and in detail. The only savior I needed was one who'd rescue me from these foes and punish them.

"There was something else, too. I didn't really believe in prayer. It felt unnatural and unreal. God was more remote than near when I recited prayers, which was only at Mass. I rarely considered praying by myself.

"And of course, like many Catholics today, I didn't believe in the Real Presence of Christ in the Eucharist."

And you wonder why I suggested that she start by going to confession?

But to her credit—and thanks to God's grace—she persisted. We met periodically for some time. I encouraged her to continue her religious education by reading some good books, and she did. But, as she recalls it, something else mattered more.

"I think you knew that what I needed was not to engage in debate. Usually, you didn't respond point by point to my religious commentary (or personal whining). But you always said something, and normally it was short and had to do with prayer and the sacraments—and suffering. Sometimes it was profitably ambiguous."

Lydia's story doesn't have a fairy-tale happy ending. It is, after all, a work in progress. Still, up to this point in time at least, things are going pretty well.

"Who could have foreseen", she asks today, "that instead of my husband becoming a convert, I would? I thank God that the best thing, and the only thing, that could have helped me through this darkness has ironically and providentially begun. You summed it all up in your latest e-mail: 'Live, Jesus, in my heart.' "

Do you have someone like Lydia in your family, in your office, living down the street? Remember: these people are our brothers and sisters in the faith, one with us in Christ. Whether or not they know it and admit it, they need and deserve our help—yours and mine.

Ecumenism and Evangelization

Protestants are, in the nature of things, diverse. History explains why. For Protestants have been busy endlessly dividing and subdividing ever since the Reformation. This can make generalizations difficult, but some things nevertheless are clear. In fact, the Catholic converts from Protestantism themselves often have striking insights to share regarding their former religious allegiance.

"I was happy to come into the Church", writes Mike, a former Methodist who is an attorney and social activist in Washington. "I saw it as a fulfillment, not a rejection, of my Methodist heritage. But for the lust of Henry VIII, after all, John Wesley would have been born in the Catholic Church. And if he had been, I imagine he would have founded a great religious order."

Already I can hear the objections beginning. "What about ecumenism?" someone is getting ready to ask. "Isn't it contrary to the friendly relations we're supposed to have with our Protestant friends to try to make Catholics of them? Aren't their churches valid expressions of Christianity too?"

That deserves an honest answer.

Start with liberal Protestantism—the familiar mainstream churches of the United States. The fact is that, like it or not, liberal Protestantism is fading fast. These denominations have been losing members for decades. Their official creeds are weak and virtually indistinguishable from one another. Where moral issues involving marriage, family, and sexuality are concerned, most of them long ago caved in. Certainly the members of these churches are generous, decent people in many ways. But as a culture-forming force in America, liberal, mainstream Protestantism is finished.

The Evangelicals and fundamentalists are a different story. Their numbers are growing, and their faith—at least, their faith in the Bible (privately interpreted, of course) as the sole source of revelation and salvation—is often very, very strong. Many of them are commendably committed prolifers and defenders of traditional marriage. As such, they merit the admiration and imitation of Catholics.

But a Christianity without sacraments, liturgy, and a living Magisterium lacks the essentials required for a true renewal of Christianity in our country, besides lacking crucial elements of what individual persons need for the following of Jesus Christ. Much as we may respect the Evangelicals, we shouldn't write them off as potential Catholics on the grounds that they're doing fine where they are. On the contrary, the Church has what many of these people are looking for and desperately need.

Orthodoxy? Pope John Paul II poured himself out in the quest for Catholic-Orthodox reunion, and Pope Benedict XVI has picked up where he left off. I hope and pray that reunion will be a reality soon. But meanwhile there are the individual Orthodox. These are Christians who belong to churches that, despite the beauty of their liturgy, their adherence to traditional creeds, and their sacraments, nevertheless have no evangelizing zeal and no meaningful spirituality for lay people in the world. It would be wrong for Catholics to turn their backs on them and walk away, saying, in effect, "Wait for reunion—whenever it finally comes."

In case you wonder—I'm in favor of ecumenism. But too often "ecumenism" gets equated with endless dialogue among nice people leading nowhere. The emphasis of the dialogue is on what we share rather than what separates us. Of course there's nothing wrong with that in itself—*but it isn't evangelization*. And evangelization is central to the mission of the Church and to our participation in that mission.

Let ecumenical dialogue continue, but let Catholic evangelization continue, too. And let us hope that, with time and grace, the spirit of authentic ecumenism will lead to unity of belief and sacramental life under one pastor.

Of Episcopalians and Evangelicals

If you've worked with enough converts over a long enough stretch of time, some patterns start to emerge according to their particular religious backgrounds. By way of illustration, let me speak of two groups, the Anglicans and the Evangelicals.

I have met many Episcopalians—now, in most cases, former Episcopalians—who were deeply saddened by developments in the church they loved that have been occurring during the last several decades. That is not a statement of Roman Catholic triumphalism. As everybody knows, the Catholic Church has had, and still has, her own share of well-publicized problems, and not a few Catholics have crossed over to the Episcopal (or Anglican) church because they find it less demanding.

But for the most part our problems have been those caused by the unsanctioned evil behavior of individuals. By contrast, the Episcopalian collapse has been a collapse of doctrinal conviction and teaching authority, often leading to the *sanctioning* of behavior that should have been condemned. As one lifelong Episcopalian, now a Roman Catholic, remarks, the temptation to which so many of his former coreligionists have succumbed is summed up in the word "sentimentality".

A British economist who teaches at a major American university tells this story.

"When I was at school I was a member of a very sincere Anglican Evangelical Bible-reading group, but by chance I started to read Cardinal Newman—the *Apologia pro Vita Sua*—first. He was worried about issues very different from the concerns of a 1970s Evangelical student group, which agonized about things like the right attitude to study and how to get out of bed punctually. His sense of the importance of continuity and authority seemed much more profound, but I couldn't at the time say why.

"As an undergraduate at Cambridge, I found that the teacher who moved me most, and who had the deepest sense of history, was a great admirer of Newman. He left Cambridge in 1978 to train as a priest in Rome and is now based at Newman's Birmingham Oratory.

"The second line of providential guidance in my life came from a sense of what was happening in Eastern Europe. I was in Czechoslovakia in August 1978, when Pope Paul VI died and the churches were draped in black. Again, without being able to say why, I was deeply moved when a Polish cardinal, obviously of great spirituality and dedication to our Lady, became Pope.

"On my first visit to Poland, in 1984, I went to Cracow at a time when Solidarity was illegal, and saw a wonderful—though small-scale—miracle.

"There was a great procession that brought thousands of people to the big market square outside St. Mary's Church. Blaring away in the square was an electronically amplified folkloric band, obviously stationed there by the Communists. As the last people crowded into the church, with me at the tail end, I looked back over the now-empty square and saw a bolt of lightning blow up the band's amplifying system.

"I met and married a girl who was the embodiment of Polish Catholic spirituality. After our first son, Maximilian, was born, the former religious dean of Peterhouse, an Anglican priest, visited us and asked how we were raising Max.

"'Catholic', we said. 'Good', he replied. 'The Catholics are just like us, except that they believe it.'

"When my wife introduced me to Father McCloskey, who tells his friends to read Newman, I knew it was time to acknowledge the truth."

Many ex-Episcopalians tell similar stories. Bronson had been a Presbyterian, but, "searching for answers and a fullness of faith that I found lacking" in that denomination, he entered the Episcopal church, as did his wife and children.

"I immediately gravitated to the Anglo-Catholic side", he recalls. "I remember a priest commenting, 'Bronson, you may have been born a Calvinist, but you have an Anglican soul.' We loved our conservative parish, and religion became an important part of our family life.

"Unfortunately, the Episcopal church was changing rapidly in radical ways. Our traditionalist faith was no longer acceptable to the national church. The theological nihilism was painful for me as I watched Anglicanism in the United States destroying itself.

"Ultimately, I was no longer satisfied with architecture, music, and ceremony. I started to think the unthinkable—becoming a Roman Catholic, or 'Roman', to use a term common in Anglo-Catholic circles.

"I truly thought of myself as a Catholic and believed I was practicing the faith. But I knew I was doing it in the wrong church. As time went by, the absurdity of belonging to a church composed of Unitarians dressed up like Catholics became undeniable."

Bronson came to see me at Mercer House in Princeton. One Sunday, as he and his son were driving to an Episcopalian church in New York, the boy told him, "Dad, I don't want to be an Episcopalian any more. I just don't get anything out of it. I think I want to be a Catholic." And Bronson replied, "You know, I don't get anything out of it any more either. Let's become Catholics together."

Father and son were received into the Church in a small ceremony in the oratory at Mercer House. "When you said at Mass that my son and I would be receiving communion for the *first* time," Bronson says, "the fact that I agreed was proof that I had really made the leap."

His wife and their other son took a little longer, but now they are Catholics, too. The young man had once considered being an Episcopal priest. He loved theology, and he had spent many hours at Mercer House discussing dogma. At his confirmation the priest joked, "He is now received into the Roman Catholic Church after a mere four hundred hours of instruction."

Evangelicals and the Authority Problem

Evangelicals are another story. Different issues come up with them as they make their way into the Church.

Among these, the central issue may be authority. It's a big problem for many of these good people. I don't mean that they are unruly or undisciplined or anything like that. I simply mean that, officially at least, the only religious authority they recognize is the Bible, as it is interpreted by each individual for himself.

Not surprisingly, the difficulties with this position are often recognized by intelligent Evangelicals themselves. And eventually that helps lead some of them to the Church. A former Evangelical named Don describes it this way: "In my early journey of faith I had been on *sola scriptura*—the Bible alone. As I probed more, however, I discovered that Scripture couldn't be the only answer.

"So much of God, for instance, is conveyed also in nature and natural law. And I came to understand the importance of tradition for handing down not just what is written but what is spoken and seen as well.

"If at school we willingly grant authority to professors by virtue of their learning and experience, then how much more logical in matters of religion to grant authority to the learning and experience of the Church. I studied the idea of papal infallibility, found it reasonable, and concluded that it was correct.

"It was getting harder, but I was still a Protestant."

The Eucharist and the other sacraments finally pushed Don over the edge—and into the Catholic Church.

Something quite different started Peggy on the way. Her story dramatizes the fact that C. S. Lewis' warning (in the story of his conversion, *Surprised by Joy*) should be taken seriously: "A young man who wishes to remain a sound atheist cannot be too careful of his reading. There are traps everywhere. . . . God is, if I may say it, very unscrupulous."

Evangelical Protestants also should watch what they read. Here's how Peggy remembers it: "On a crisp autumn day I left my office in downtown Washington for a lunch-hour walk. I happened to pass by a small Catholic bookstore I'd never noticed before. I was short on time, but I thought I'd run in and buy a copy of William Bennett's *The Children's Book of Virtues* for my son.

"Having grown up an Evangelical Protestant, I was reluctant to go into a Catholic bookstore. 'All those schlocky beads and candy-colored statues!' I thought. But I went in anyway, found the book, and was headed for the cash register. Then a display of interesting books caught my eye.

"I picked up one called *Surprised by Truth*—stories about Protestants and others who'd converted to Catholicism. The title was hokey, but the book looked intriguing. 'Why on earth', I asked myself, 'would a Protestant, especially an Evangelical minister, convert to Catholicism?' As I thumbed through the book, I was shocked to come across arguments for crossing the Tiber that my Protestant upbringing had shielded me from.

"I bought both books and left the bookstore. I was exhilarated at the thought of a new intellectual challenge—considering the claims of Catholicism and finding them lacking, as any serious Protestant surely would do."

You will not be surprised to learn that she didn't. The cashier at the bookstore—it was the Catholic Information Center, of course—tossed in a reprint of an article I'd written called "Seven Daily Habits of Holy, Apostolic People". It recommended the basics—daily Mass, prayer morning and evening, Scripture reading, the Rosary.

Peggy read it. Now she recalls, "I couldn't deny the very powerful sense of God's presence and direction I felt. I knew the Lord was speaking to me in an unexpected, personal way, in answer to my prayers for my son and for my family's spiritual life.

"The message was hard for Protestant ears, but as a Protestant I was tired of hitting my head on the shallow end of Christian faith too many times. I could see that the goal of

Christian life was intimate, ever-deepening union with the Lord. But I'd worked for some of Evangelicalism's leading lights, and I couldn't see how to get there with my Protestant resources."

Then she read another article that the cashier also had included—one on spiritual direction.

"If it's a good idea for Catholics, I reasoned, it must be a good idea for Protestants. I summoned all the courage I could muster and called the brochure's author to ask if he would give direction to a Protestant.

"But I called on Sunday evening, knowing he would hardly be there. Almost hyperventilating, I left a message on the voicemail—and I hoped I'd done my duty in response to God's call, and through no fault of mine this priest would never call back.

"You did."

Just as, I like to think, any priest—or Catholic lay person—would have done.

As she recalls, when she came to see me, I started by saying that the Catholic Church is fundamentally about "a relationship with Jesus". Then I recommended that she read Frank Sheed's fine book *To Know Christ Jesus*.

As an Evangelical Protestant, she thought she already knew a lot about Christ. Didn't Evangelicals know Scripture backward and forward, after all? But she read the book anyway. And over time she read a lot of other books—about *sola scriptura* and *sola fide*, about the primacy of the Pope, the role of Mary, transubstantiation, confession, and much else.

"I took my time with them," Peggy reports, "meditated on what I read, wrestled with the arguments, prayed, cried, spoke with friends on both sides of the divide, and attended Mass for more than a year."

But in the end it was the first book—Sheed's *To Know Christ Jesus*—that did the trick.

"The chapter entitled 'Mainly about Bread', which explains the sixth chapter of John and the Eucharist from the Catholic perspective, was so clear, so utterly convincing, and so breathtaking in its implications, that I knew I would never see Communion or the Catholic Church the same way again."

Now Peggy is a convinced, contented Catholic. C. S. Lewis was right—be careful what you read.

About Non-Christians

"Non-Christians" covers a lot of ground. Most of my experience in convert work with non-Christians has been with Jews, so let me start with them.

A rather confusing discussion is taking place in Catholic theological circles today (at least, I find it confusing) about whether the Old Covenant between the Jewish people and God remains operative and whether it is still sufficient for the salvation of Jews. Don't misunderstand me—I have no doubt that Jews can be saved. The issue is where and how the Old Covenant fits in.

Now, this undoubtedly is a very interesting theological question, but in practical terms it's also a question that needn't concern most of us in dealing with Jewish friends who express an interest in the Catholic Church. Does anybody seriously imagine that it's right to tell them, "Sorry, but you're the Chosen People, and the Old Covenant is good enough for you"? If Jews want to know and love and follow Jesus Christ, it is our job to give them a hand and leave the theorizing to somebody else.

Jews should not be a special target for Christian evangelization (and certainly not for proselytism in the negative sense); neither should they be cut off from hearing—and, let us hope, welcoming—the good news of Christ. We ought to share our faith with them as generously and enthusiastically as with anybody else.

It isn't easy for Jews to become Christians. They risk losing the friendship of other Jews and even being ostracized by their own families if they convert—and sometimes they may suffer in the pocketbook, too. Yet I've found many Jews open to hearing the Christian good news. That's because their many wonderful traits include a great appreciation for the Law and a resolute determination to seek the truth at all cost through serious study.

Moreover, in investigating the claims of Christianity, Jews generally take Catholicism as the gold standard of the Christian proposition—this, for better or worse, is what Christianity *really* is. And if they do become Catholics, they don't look back. Their losses in this life, whatever they may be, are counted as nothing compared with the "pearl of great price".

In modern times, the Holocaust is the great, traumatic shared experience of Judaism and Jews. And however you look at it, there is no getting away from the fact that Christians and Catholics shared part of the blame for that enormous evil. Jewish converts are smart enough to realize that doesn't invalidate the claims of the faith, but it remains an ever-present reality that needs to be faced.

The story of my Jewish friend Seymour makes that abundantly clear.

A week after he met Kathleen, the woman who was to become his wife (though neither of them knew that just then), she told him her parents were coming to town—Washington, D.C., that is—and they wanted to visit the Holocaust Museum. Her father was a charter member of the museum, but he hadn't visited it yet. Had Seymour? No. Would he like to? Yes.

"Now, this was curious", he writes. "I was being escorted to a museum that featured *my people* by Catholics who not only felt strongly about the Holocaust but were more energetic than I was in giving it their attention. I knew Jews that grieved those losses—I most certainly grieved them myself—but, naively, I didn't know that others also genuinely grieved.

"And so my journey to becoming a Catholic began."

Soon after that he made another discovery: the Catholic liturgy begins with the Old Testament and extends to the New. "It was comforting to see the Old Testament used as a building block and to understand that so many of its teachings led to Christ", he says.

"I also grasped that the dedication of the people at Mass—including Kathleen—to those teachings and to Christ was somehow one and the same. And somehow, too, not only could Kathleen's family become my *brothers and sisters*, but so could people next to me in the pew whom I'd never met."

From that point it was a short trip to Catholicism for Seymour.

And other non-Christians? Once again I hesitate to generalize, since I haven't had much experience in the convert line with them. In principle, of course, there's no reason why Muslims, Hindus, Buddhists, and all the rest shouldn't hear the message of Christ and respond. And indeed some have. Yet the obstacles to evangelization are obviously very great, especially in Muslim countries like Saudi Arabia, where Christianity is kept under very tight wraps and barely tolerated at all.

Short of some spectacular divine intervention, then, it seems pretty clear that the only form of effective apostolate with Muslims has *got* to be one by one, family by family, and that friendship will be the key. Perhaps the prospects will improve as Muslims and Christians more and more meet and interact in the United States and other countries of the West.

If I'm short on experience with Muslims, Hindus, and Buddhists, though, at least I can share with you the recollections of Joel the Jewish Sikh—now a Roman Catholic. Joel writes, "I grew up in a nonpracticing Jewish home in an overwhelmingly Christian neighborhood. My first awareness of Christ came from the taunts of neighborhood kids pointing out that (a) I didn't believe in Christ and (b) I somehow bore responsibility for his death.

"I had some training in Judaism, but I never bothered to get a bar mitzvah. Neither my parents nor I were interested in pursuing a religious education. And yet I was deeply interested in things spiritual. I majored in religion in college—A in Eastern religions, C in Christianity and Judaism. The department head invited me to change my major. I took her advice.

"After college my religious instincts surfaced, and I joined an ashram where yoga and the Sikh religion were practiced. Soon after, I married. My first three years with the ashram were happy, the last twelve were ... not. But for the sake of my marriage, I stayed.

"Eventually, though, I couldn't take it anymore. I left. Fortunately, my marriage and my family survived. But my wife is still a member of the group."

One day a broker in Joel's investment firm invited him to lend a hand with a nonprofit organization dedicated to helping the Church in Russia. It was headed by a priest whom Joel liked.

Over dinner he asked the priest, "What does God expect from me, a man who practices no religion and got burned by bad religious choices?"

"God expects you to learn about him", the priest answered.

Joel buckled down to do that. Eventually, his priest friend was transferred. He referred Joel to me, and we resumed work. Joel goes on, "One day I asked, 'How long does it take until one is baptized?' Your answer was, 'It could be months, or it could be ten years.'

"Ten years. That seemed excessive. At our next meeting I said, 'How about if we just move on to the baptism?' You said, 'Okay.' "

And we did.

"I've been a Catholic for three years now", concludes the Jewish Sikh. "The Father, Son, and Holy Spirit are the central reality of my existence now.

"Nothing has changed in my life except . . . everything. I can't explain that. Anyone who believes will understand. I've been given the opportunity to enter into friendship with the Divine through the commitment of dedicated priests. How fortunate I am! I was lost. Now, by the grace of God, I am found."

VII

A Handy-Dandy How-to-Do-It Kit

I hope it's clear that the title of this chapter is meant to be funny. There is no handy-dandy kit for producing conversions. A chapter title like this one simply gives me an opportunity to underline that point.

Authentic conversion is the work of God's grace. Grace works in countless different ways suited to the circumstances of the individuals to whom God offers it. Many of those ways are surprising, not to say profoundly mysterious, to those of us who look at them with merely human eyes. "Why would God do it like *that*?" we say. Believe me—God knows what he's doing.

As an instance of the odd way grace operates, consider the man who reports that God's call came to him as he was exercising on a treadmill.

To pass the time, he was watching EWTN, and it had an effect. "EWTN reinvigorated my old interest in Catholicism," he says, "and that started me reading the Gospels and Catholic apologetics in depth. If I ever write a book about all this, I'm going to call it *The Treadmill to Damascus* instead of *The Road to Damascus*."

Then there's the woman whose nonbelieving Jewish father took her as a child to visit St. Patrick's Cathedral in New York. What on earth moved her father to do that? I suppose he saw the trip simply as an outing. Almost certainly it didn't occur to him that he was giving an opening to God.

Of course the little girl didn't become a Catholic on the spot—that happened only many years later, when she was a grown woman. But that early visit to St. Patrick's stuck in her memory over all those years, and she looks back on it now as an important turning point. "I somehow was aware that God was there", she explains.

The Importance of Friendship

If there's any factor that turns up over and over in conversion stories, it's the role played by the converts' contacts with Catholic friends. I've made this point earlier, but it is so important that it's worth pausing and reflecting on it at some length.

To be able to evangelize is a privilege and a joy for any Christian. Success in this enterprise is relative. We evangelize out of love, without keeping track of numbers. Only in heaven will we know and rejoice in the many ways that God has used us to bring souls to him. (And, to be frank about it, we also may find ourselves spending more time in Purgatory than we expected because of all the opportunities we either missed or spoiled by our laziness, cowardice, or bad example.)

Example is crucial, and good example involves paying attention to small details—or, rather, to details that may seem small, but which really aren't. A clean, well-groomed, well-spoken person visibly possessing the human virtues—things like friendliness, good humor, patience, loyalty, truthfulness—is more humanly attractive and more likely to make and influence friends than . . . but you can fill in the rest for yourself.

At the same time, however, we would be proud as serpents if we came to imagine that how we look or act or what we say will ultimately bring people to Christ. You and I can help get the ball rolling, so to speak, and keep it moving in the right direction. But that's all we can do.

And yet it's also very much. It doesn't come out of a spiritual vacuum. Effective evangelization must flow from prayer and mortification and participation in the sacraments—from one's own ongoing ascetical struggle to put on Jesus Christ.

Someone may ask: What about the media? They are tremendously important, of course, sometimes for good and sometimes for ill. Our own times have witnessed the greatest revolution in communications since the invention of the printing press in the fifteenth century, and it's still under way. People speak of the "global village". But thanks to cell phones and the Internet, we also are well along in creating a media-based global communion of saints that can be likened to the spiritual communion of the saints we profess in the Creed.

Programs and materials for evangelization and catechesis have multiplied, and in many cases they are available free or almost free on the Internet. (Be sure to take a look at the Vatican Web site—vatican.va—as an invaluable source for documents presenting the teaching of the Catholic Church. There also are many other excellent Catholic Web sites as well.)

And there are Catholic TV and radio networks, as well as thousands of Catholic publishing houses, magazines, and newspapers. The sheer quantity of media that can be used for evangelization and catechesis is astonishing. But be warned: quantity isn't always quality, and it isn't safe to assume that some program or book or magazine is orthodox just because it carries the name "Catholic". If in doubt, seek reliable advice. The fundamental point, though, is that it's extremely easy to find material these days, and much of it is very good.

The Importance of One-on-One

But all of it, good as it is, will never take the place of the personal, one-on-one (and, sometimes, family-to-family) relationships that are at the heart of evangelization and conversion. Evangelization always involves a personal relationship of love expressed in the evangelizer's gift of self.

Note that this can be an unconscious, spontaneous gift. The story of Lydia—we saw some of it in the last chapter—illustrates that.

"When I was in third grade we spent part of a year in the Washington, D.C., area. Even in 1964 Silver Spring, Maryland, had a more diverse population than many other places. There were Catholics! I'd never known any before. Jews and Catholics together then constituted only about 4 percent of the population of North Carolina, where I grew up.

"A little friend of mine from our apartment complex invited me for dinner. I'd never before seen a crucifix in a home. I'd never been around anyone who prayed grace making the sign of the Cross. It was mysterious and appealing.

"My parents, always diligent about sightseeing, took my brother and me to see the Shrine of the Immaculate Conception. What a contrast it was to the bare simplicity of Southern Baptist sanctuaries. All those statues, the art, stained glass, candles, chapels, holy water! There were people on their knees in the pews praying—and there wasn't even a service going on at the time!

"A year later, back in North Carolina, I met Mary, a girl my age—about ten, that is. With her two older brothers, she rode a Trailways bus to the next town to attend a Catholic school. I rode the same bus to go to a nonsectarian private school in the same town.

"There was something about those kids that intrigued me. Mary, Mark, and Matthew wore uniforms. They were quiet and well behaved. I could see that their parents were making sacrifices to send them to a Catholic school. They all had saints' names. I had no idea what a saint was, but at least I understood that it meant these children were somehow linked to special Christians.

"I wanted to be Mary's friend. She came over several times. We never discussed points of doctrine, but something about her and her family conveyed an age-appropriate message about the goodness of Catholic life."

Somehow I doubt that ten-year-old Mary thought of herself as an evangelizer. But she was.

How about teachers? They, too, can play enormously important roles. And they can do it without in any way violating their professional, academic role or overstepping the boundaries of the teacher-student relationship. They can do it simply by being conscientious and good at their job.

Take the case of a young woman named Madeleine, a recent graduate of an elite university.

"Although I was raised as a Protestant," she says, "I went to a well-known Catholic school because *U.S. News and World Report* gave it a good rating.

"I thought of myself as a serious Christian, but all I really wanted out of life was material security. I studied a lot of nonsense in my first few semesters, biding my time until I could take my diploma to law school or out into the working world, and there make a great deal of money.

"Things took a different turn in my junior year. One of my professors was a wise old priest who was an orthodox Catholic. He was one of the few teachers on that campus who was. Under his tutelage I read St. Thomas Aquinas for the first time—specifically, the questions in the *Summa Theologiae* that deal with natural law.

"I was utterly fascinated by that idea of order that St. Thomas presents. The fact that all things have their proper functioning and that it tends toward God, our ultimate end, captivated me.

"I came to see that the Catholic Church has a coherent, systematic explanation along these lines that explains how a Christian should order his life. In contrast, the Protestant faith I'd grown up with offered a confused, fragmented view of human activity. Often it boiled down to, 'If you can back it up with a Bible verse, go for it.'

"My conversion to Catholicism was primarily an intellectual one", Madeleine notes. No doubt it was. Thanks in large part to St. Thomas Aquinas and a wise old orthodox priest professor.

Getting Started

As was suggested earlier, one good way of beginning is to begin.

The question "Have you ever thought of becoming a Catholic?" is at least guaranteed to get a person's attention, and it may also start him thinking and, either now or in the future, lead to positive results. As I pointed out, this is a question to ask a friend or someone who's on the way to becoming your friend. Friendship, either real or incipient, is essential, lest the question make the other party feel threatened or annoyed.

It also can start the other way around—the other person approaches you. To repeat something else that was said above, this obviously is far more likely to happen if you give him reason for doing it through your looks, your speech, and your way of dressing and behaving.

I don't mean you should act like a plaster saint. That's far more likely to repel than to attract. I mean acting like a decent, normal human being who is just like everybody else, except.... Someone not given to telling off-color jokes or engaging in sexual innuendo and petty gossip. Someone who doesn't goof off on the job but instead tries to help others with a kindly word and a pat on the back. A person who in a quiet yet visible way gives evidence of being in love with the Catholic faith—by keeping a little picture of the Blessed Virgin on his desk, for instance, or by going to Mass not just on Sundays but on weekdays when that's possible, or by doing other such things that come naturally to a believing, practicing Catholic.

Now, let's suppose such behavior—natural and unaffected, but not exactly run-of-the-mill—does raise certain questions in somebody else's mind. He likes what he sees, he feels curiously attracted by it, he wants to learn more. The initial conversation might go something like this.

Frank says, "Joe, we've been working together several months, and I can't help noticing that you seem to be a serious Catholic. I wonder if you could spare a few minutes over lunch or coffee so I can talk to you about that.

"I was raised a kind of lukewarm Christian myself, but somehow I have this feeling I should be taking religion more seriously. My wife and I both have noticed that our kids have started asking questions—I mean, questions about God and all that—which we just can't answer. I think they get it from other kids in the neighborhood.

"Also, to tell you the truth, we're both kind of uncomfortable about stuff that's going on in the world. Anytime you think TV can't get worse, it does, and that's not the only problem. The Catholic Church seems to have some answers, and I'm curious what they are.

"Now, don't misunderstand me—I'm not planning to become a Catholic. With all due respect, I know lots of things about the Catholic Church that I don't like. But I have some questions anyway that I'd like to ask. So, what do you say?"

Joe says, "Thanks for bringing it up, Frank. I like working with you, and I'll be glad to help you any way I can. Let's have lunch next Tuesday, as you suggest. And if that goes well, maybe we can get together every month or so to talk about where Christ fits in a guy's life and where the Church comes in.

"I'm no preacher, but I'll try to answer your questions as best I can, and if you're interested I can recommend some good books for you and your wife to read. But keep this in mind—by and large, I'm in the same boat you are, looking for answers and trying to live the best life I can with results that aren't always so great.

"I understand you're just curious now. I'm not going to try to make a Catholic out of you. But I have to be honest and say I don't think it's an accident that you said to me what you just said. God has something in mind here for both of us. I'm going to be praying for you and your wife between now and Tuesday.

"Oh, by the way, who do you like in the Redskins-Giants game?"

Curing the Friendship Deficit

A serious and potentially deadly epidemic is sweeping the United States. I call it the friendship deficit syndrome (FDS). This ailment is a major obstacle to evangelization. For that reason, and many others as well, we need to work out a new and better approach to being friends in America. It should be one that is distinctively American and respects the real strengths in American culture.

Although my emphasis here is on friendship as a vehicle for evangelization, it's essential to understand that friendship is a precious thing in itself, something to be sought and cherished for its own sake. Instrumentalizing friendship is a dreadful abuse of this precious thing. By instrumentalizing it, I mean turning it into a platform or mere means for getting ahead, making a sale, winning votes, or accomplishing anything else—including evangelizing.

Given that fundamental principle, though, it's also a fact that genuine friendship is an all but indispensable part of the process of evangelization and conversion.

If you're a woman, I ask your pardon for concentrating on men when I talk about friendship. It goes without saying that women also need to have friends and be friends. But I truly believe that here and now the friendship deficit syndrome is a much bigger problem for American men than it is for American women.

At the same time, I recommend that women who care about men—mothers, sisters, wives, and prospective wives—pay close attention to what follows. Besides concern for the man or men in their life, self-interest dictates that. In the absence of strong men capable of entering into and sustaining healthy relationships—including friendships with other men—marriage and the family are at risk. And when marriage and family crumble, women and children are bound to be the big losers.

Wives especially can help combat FDS by encouraging their husbands to spend more time, not less, with their male friends. Yes, you heard me right—more time, not less.

I realize perfectly well that women who work outside the home while at the same time having domestic chores understandably want their husbands home as much as possible in the evenings and on weekends—for companionship and also to help with the work. But if a wife insists that her husband *always* be at home when he isn't at work, she may be denying him the opportunity to become a better husband and father by learning how to be a better friend. In concrete, individual circumstances, striking just the right balance in the allocation of the man's time is a problem I can't presume to resolve for any particular couple. I can only say that it has to be done.

For many contemporary Americans, loneliness may be the greatest affliction, and FDS may be at the heart of it. The title of a much-discussed book a few years ago got it just right: *Bowling Alone.* True, the syndrome has many causes: small families resulting from contraception and abortion; absent spouses (attributable to divorce and also to the economic pressure put on wives to work outside the home in the absence of a truly family-friendly tax system); frequent moves that make it difficult for people to put down roots (often the result of corporate policies that place profit above the interests of families); attaching more value to material possessions than to human relationships; the worship of youth.

Somebody once said the average American man has "one good friend, and that is his wife". It is essential for a wife to be her husband's friend, of course—but his *only* good friend? Surely not. That reflects the individualism of a culture still shaped in many ways by the legacy of the country's Protestant past.

Popular culture cherishes two ideal images of the American man. One is the image of the isolated male figure riding off into the sunset by himself. As he goes, he is leaving relationships behind. He hides his feelings behind a crusty exterior and feigns indifference to the rest of the world. He answers to his own conscience and to nobody and nothing else. And side by side with this image is another: the fast-talking, wise-cracking, woman-ogling American man on the make.

Two movie icons—John Wayne and Bob Hope—epitomized these versions of the American male in the not-so-distant past. (Interestingly enough, both ended their days turning to the Catholic Church.) Neither image is an adequate expression of authentic masculinity.

In saying that, however, I surely don't wish to imply that the feminization of men—something now visibly occurring on all sides—is the answer. "Getting in touch with your feelings", whatever that means, may possibly be a good idea, but it shouldn't mean turning men into weaklings. A far better way of expressing what's needed is the phrase "gift of self", originating with the Second Vatican Council and often repeated by that model of Catholic manhood, Pope John Paul II. And while the gift of self is given primarily in and through holy matrimony, it also takes place in a man's friendships with other men.

In today's America, that isn't so easy. Apart from participation in a few sports (and even that traditional male bastion is now subject to female encroachment), many young men have very little opportunity to enjoy exclusively male companionship. Laws, social policies, and cultural pressures combine to make that increasingly difficult to do. The decline in single-sex high schools and colleges complicates the task. Many formerly all-male clubs and organizations are now open to women. So are the ranks of Catholic altar servers (no longer called altar *boys*). Even the military services are becoming more and more sexually integrated—sometimes with disastrous results, including the sexual promiscuity that any reasonable person might have expected from a practice that represents the triumph of ideology over good sense.

The problem extends beyond the teens and twenties. It is increasingly rare for a man in the course of his career to work for only one or two employers. But job hopping impedes the formation of lasting friendships as former colleagues and fellow workers are abandoned—or in some cases become competitors. The extraordinary physical mobility of American families impedes the development of neighborhood and parish relationships capable of blossoming into friendships. Above all, the widespread breakup of families by separation and divorce deprives young boys at a crucial time in their lives of virtuous male role models—conscientious fathers, that is—and impairs their emotional capacity for friendship.

As it stands, for many men—Catholics along with the rest—"friendship" has come to signify an attenuated and largely artificial tie based on little more than a common interest in beer, cars, sports, and/or the promiscuous pursuit of young women. By contrast, a genuine male friendship is a deep and lasting bond that reaches to the two friends' depths. Such friendships are not common among American men today.

In present-day America yet another reason for that concerns the fact that many male relationships are openly homosexual. That is to say, they are relationships based on mutual exploitation of each by the other as a source of pleasure. Movies, books, television, and plays now present homosexuality as normal, perhaps even desirable, and actively propagandize the rest of us to buy into that fiction.

One unhappy side effect of the marketing of the gay lifestyle is that, especially in big cities, two men or a small group of men seen socializing with each other in a public place are likely to draw stares from others and the unspoken question "I wonder if they're gay." In these circumstances many heterosexual men skip the hassles and the embarrassment by not socializing much with other men.

Finding a Cure For FDS

What to do?

Resisting this tidal wave of social pathology is enormously difficult, but resistance is necessary for many reasons—including the reestablishment and defense of male friendship as a basis for evangelization and apostolate.

Pope John Paul points out that dialogue is one of the principal means of creating and sustaining a friendship. There can be no friendship without communication—a conversation of some sort, whether spoken or written. Where it's a matter of evangelization, apostolate, and conversion, this calls for a serious, conscious, personal commitment on the part of a Christian—in this case, a Christian man—to share his faith with his neighbors, colleagues, companions, fellow workers, and associates of all kinds in the varied settings of his life.

In trying to size up one's own friendship deficit syndrome, it might be well to conduct a kind of FDS inventory, along the following lines:

—How many true friends do I have?

—How many would lay down their lives for me—and I for them?

—How many men do I know to whom I can open up my heart in total trust?

—If I were to die today, how many would deeply care?

—How many people's lives have I changed in a positive way by being their friend?

—How many have been converted to or reconciled with the Church or grown in their practice of their faith as a result of being my friend?

—Are my friends and my friendships a central part of my prayer life? Do I talk about my friends—pleading for their needs, trying to understand them better and see more clearly how I can help them—with the one who is Best Friend of us all?

Let me close these reflections on friendship with the testimonials of some converts who've experienced what friendship can do.

Jeff: "A friend suggested I attend an Opus Dei retreat. That retreat sealed the deal."

Barbara: "A good friend of mine suggested I come with her on retreat and just see what it was like."

Don: "When I tell of my spiritual sojourn, I speak fondly of those who discipled me early on. Out in Hong Kong there was a Mr. D, a Mr. G, and a Mr. E. Without them I would not have come to know Christ."

Julian: "When I interned in D.C., some of my fellow interns encouraged me to come to church, and I was open to it, in part because thoughts about death and marriage were beginning to make me look for a real purpose to things. More and more, the friends and role models I met were Catholics, and many, including my boss, were converts."

Angela: "I barely understood anything Ted said. But it is extremely scary to convert, and I knew full well that my family would be stunned, disbelieving, and doubtful. I knew I would open myself to gossip, lose some friends, and be dismissed as having a midlife crisis. Ted offered me lifelines to get me through the struggle."

Perhaps second in importance only to God's grace, friendship is a central ingredient in countless conversions. Be a true friend. Help your friends find Christ.

VIII

Apologetics for Evangelization

The men and women whom I've been fortunate enough to accompany on their journeys to the Catholic faith are a remarkable and highly diverse group of human beings.

They include Protestant ministers, prominent business and professional people, well-known intellectuals, politicians, journalists, even the head of a synagogue. And of course they also include many people who might be described as ordinary individuals, except that they are truly extraordinary—as everybody is, once you get to know them.

In my experience, the "celebrity" converts have several things in common. All of them are people of high intelligence. All have a voracious appetite for books and, most important, an all-consuming thirst for the truth in religious matters.

In becoming Catholics, many of these people faced opposition from their families, potential damage to their reputations, and the risk of harm to their careers. But the conviction that they had found the pearl of great price, the one true Church founded by Jesus Christ, which now continues to serve as his agent and indeed as his very presence in the world, drove them on. Their assent to truth was not what John Henry Newman might have called merely notional; it was intensely, dynamically real.

Know Your History

The historical argument played a powerful role in these conversions. In working with these people, I made it a habit to insist that they read several books on the history of the Catholic Church. To me, the historical argument for Catholicism is rationally unassailable: either the Lord of History established a Church with a visible structure that will remain until he comes again—and that Church is the Roman Catholic Church—or else there is no religious authority present in the world that must be obeyed. As one of the converts puts it today, "As one who had studied church history, I saw that only the Catholic Church could claim to be in continuity with the Apostles." It's a powerful argument.

The men and women whom I've instructed in the faith during these twenty years have read Philip Hughes, Christopher Dawson, Ronald Knox, G.K. Chesterton, Robert Hugh Benson, Louis Bouyer, Orestes Brownson, and Warren Carroll, along with others. They also have read anthologies of convert stories. History, I believe, is at the heart of all conversions—both personal histories and history as it is written by the historians (including even Flavius Josephus, Pliny the Younger, the Venerable Bede, and people more or less hostile to Catholicism like Gibbon and Macaulay).

We also need to understand the present moment—and in order to do that, we have to see the present in historical perspective. Some parts of the contemporary world are living in a post-Christian era. That is especially true of Europe and parts of North America. Even though this pains Christians, it shouldn't surprise them. In earlier times, Christianity all but disappeared in some other regions—for example, the Middle East and North Africa after the Islamic conquest.

Now an even more rapid and unsettling de-Christianization appears to be taking place in Europe. It is marked by minimal or nonexistent religious practice on the part of many; the collapse of traditional morality and its replacement by the morality of "choice"; and what now resembles a continent-wide demographic suicide by contraception, sterilization, and abortion. Never fear—the faith will survive. But there is no guarantee it will survive everywhere in Europe.

And the United States? Liberal Protestantism is fading fast. Virtually all the so-called mainstream churches have long since caved in on issues relating to marriage, family, and sex. To take just one especially conspicuous case, the Episcopal Church USA seems bent on destroying itself in the great cause of defending sodomy.

Looking to the sector of Protestantism that lies to the right of center, I have great respect for Evangelicals and fundamentalists who take the Bible seriously as the sole norm of faith. But a version of Christianity without the sacraments, without liturgy, and without teaching authority hardly will be in a position to accomplish a renewal of Christian life and the successful evangelization of culture in the United States.

Like it or not, friends, it's up to us Roman Catholics. There's nobody else around to do the job that needs doing. And without excluding the possibility that, by some miracle of God's grace, mass conversions—of whole groups or even of whole denominations—might lie ahead, I have no hesitation in saying that as far into the future as anyone can see, and certainly for our lifetimes, people will come to the fullness of faith one by one, sometimes family by family, and here and there perhaps congregation by congregation. And only in that way.

During the last three decades, the magnificent witness of one man—Pope John Paul II—drew an untold number of newcomers to the Catholic Church and encouraged many lapsed or lukewarm Catholics to return. This man was an enormous gift—an enormous grace—from God. Two other factors also are helping to break through the wall of mistrust, misunderstanding, and ignorance in this post-Christian time and place.

One is the rise of new ecclesial institutions and movements whose impact is just now beginning to be felt in our country. Operating with the full approval of the Church, these heavily lay groups are by their very nature apostolic and evangelizing. Their visible testimony of Catholic Christianity lived out in the world may in time draw millions to the Church.

The other is the large and rapidly growing number of Hispanic Catholics. Without them, the United States, like Europe, would now be experiencing demographic suicide—losing population, that is. Catechized and properly formed, the Hispanic newcomers represent a potential body of evangelizers large in numbers and strong in faith.

Answers and Arguments

Anyone who ventures into the business of trying to bring his friends to the faith—and every Catholic should do that—sooner or later will almost certainly find himself having to offer arguments for Catholicism. Doing apologetics, it's called.

As a matter of fact, at one point in the gestation of this book its working title was the title of this chapter: "Apologetics for Evangelization". It may not have been the greatest title in the world, but it made some sense. For even though evangelization and apologetics are two quite different things, in practice they often are very closely linked. Since someone busy "making converts" can expect to be peppered with questions, he will be well advised to have—or at least to know where to find—true and convincing answers.

That being so, it will be helpful to take a quick look here at some common questions and objections that are likely to come up, probably fairly early in the process, with someone who is thinking seriously about becoming a full-fledged member of the Church. The aim isn't to cover the waterfront or go into any of these matters in depth, but just to offer a few insights and suggestions as a starting point to help readers in their own research and reflection.

1. The Catholic Church has been responsible for all sorts of terrible things over the centuries—the Crusades, the Galileo case, and so much else. How can anybody possibly be expected to believe that a Church like this is God's Church?

"Cultish, superstitious, antiintellectual, and anti-Semitic" is how one recent convert to Catholicism describes his former image of the Catholic Church. Some converts report that their minds were systematically poisoned against Catholicism by leaders of their own churches or their coreligionists or parents.

But it would be a mistake to place all the blame on other people. The historical record of the Catholic Church is indeed mixed, to say the least. *Saints and Sinners* is the title of a popular history of the papacy by Eamon Duffy published a few years ago—and Popes are hardly the only Catholics whom that tag fits.

Pope John Paul II in the Jubilee Year 2000 made an astonishing gesture by offering a general apology—a kind of act of contrition, if you will—for the historical failures and sins of Catholics through the centuries. A "purification of memory" he called it, and it was far and away the greatest *mea culpa* ever uttered. No other religious body has ever done anything like that. Taking a leaf from the Pope's book, we need to admit our mistakes.

At the same time, we are entitled to insist that critics of the Church get their facts straight. A lot of the crimes attributed to Catholics either were not as represented, didn't occur at all, or look quite different when viewed in their historical and cultural context. (It is, to take one instance, a huge misreading of the historical record and an injustice to the memory of a great man to suggest that Pope Pius XII was friendly to Hitler or shared the blame for the Holocaust.) The Church has been the target of calumnies and slanders from the very beginning. That seems likely never to change.

In any case, the relevant measure of the Church is not her sinners. Every institution, every group—every church—has plenty of those. The measure of the Church is her saints, the men and women who with God's grace have lived up to the highest ideals of holiness as presented by Jesus in the Beatitudes.

If someone is looking for the living heart of Catholicism, let him look at Francis of Assisi, Francis Xavier, Francis de Sales, Teresa of Avila, Thérèse of Lisieux, Elizabeth Seton, Maximilian Kolbe, and Edith Stein. Let him look also and especially at those who today still seek to live as they did, as disciples and imitators of Jesus Christ. Catholicism is sinful because it's human; it can be saintly only because it's divine.

2. How can anyone possibly believe the Pope is infallible? The Pope is just a man, a fallible human being, like the rest of us.

Of course the Pope is a human being like the rest of us, and as history makes amply clear, Popes can and do make mistakes. But that's not the issue where infallibility is concerned.

Consider this. If you believe that God has revealed matters of great importance to the human race, and if you further believe—and who can doubt it?—that over time human beings inevitably confuse and distort just about any message they receive, then you must believe either of two things: (a) God revealed in vain, since his message by now must have become hopelessly confused and distorted, beyond any possibility of returning it to its original pristine condition, or (b) God did *not* reveal in vain, since he took the sensible precaution of bestowing the gift of infallibility upon his Church precisely so that revelation would be preserved and transmitted intact from generation to generation until the end of time.

Now, to that someone might reply, "You're wrong. God did all that needed to be done by committing his revelation to a written book—the Holy Bible." And I agree that the Bible truly is the word, the revelation, of God. But the painful fact is that for centuries people who believe that very thing concerning the Bible have disagreed fiercely and profoundly among themselves over what countless passages in the Bible actually mean. In reality—and I mean no disrespect in saying this—the Bible taken by itself doesn't solve the problem of preserving and transmitting God's revelation but only makes the problem worse.

So, I repeat: *if* God reveals and *if* he wants us to know for sure what he reveals, infallibility is necessary.

Note that infallibility, as Catholics understand it, is given to the Church. As the Catechism of the Catholic Church says, "In order to preserve the Church in the purity of the faith handed on by the apostles, Christ who is the Truth willed to confer on her a share in his own infallibility." Thus the faith and teaching of the Catholic Church about what God has revealed and what is necessary for salvation are infallibly correct—by a special, preservative act of God, they cannot be in error.

The infallibility of the Pope (and also the infallibility of the bishops teaching in union with the Pope, whether in a general council or dispersed throughout the world) is part of the infallibility of the Church. That is to say, when the Pope teaches infallibly, he is not just teaching something on his own—acting in isolation from everybody else, exercising a remarkable gift that is exclusively his. On the contrary, when the Pope teaches infallibly, he is teaching *what the Church infallibly believes*.

When these matters are clearly and correctly explained, many prospective converts find the idea of infallibility to be far more credible and attractive than the alternatives.

3. Catholics may not worship the Blessed Virgin, but in my opinion they come pretty close to doing so, and that's idolatry. Furthermore, many of the things Catholics believe about Mary—the Immaculate Conception, the virgin birth, the Assumption, the appearances of Mary at places like Lourdes and Fatima—strike me as superstitions and stories for children, things that a reasonable adult can't accept.

The testimony of the Christian tradition regarding Mary is ancient and compelling. Marian doctrine and Marian devotion are hardly new inventions, and this is another area where the open-minded study of history can help.

It's also important to bear in mind—as Pope John Paul repeatedly points out—that the role of Marian doctrine and devotion is to direct us to Christ. "To Jesus through Mary" is our prayer. When, for example, the Council of Ephesus in A.D. 431 solemnly taught that the Blessed Virgin is *Theotokos*—Mother of God—it was making a statement not only about Mary but also, more especially, about her Son: Jesus Christ is man *and* God.

Preeminently, though, belief and devotion regarding Mary represent an area where rational argument will take you just so far. At a certain point, love has to take over. Someone who loves Jesus Christ will naturally love his family and friends—and especially his mother.

I have much testimony on this matter from "my" converts. Yes, some of them say they had problems with Catholic beliefs about Mary—or what they *supposed* or had been *told* were Catholic beliefs, which isn't always the same thing—and sometimes the problems persisted even after they came into the Church.

That's true, for instance, with my friend Agnes, who still has her doubts about the scriptural evidence, or lack thereof, for some doctrines about Mary, but who nevertheless writes, "I believe totally in Mary; her love and sacrifice make me weep. Her prefiguring of Jesus' sacrifice, 'Not my will but thine'—brings tears to my eyes."

As that suggests, time and again newcomers to the Church have found that their new relationship with the Blessed Mother is a kind of bonus of being Catholic. And for some it was in fact Mary who helped lead them to Catholicism—as in the case of a man who among "reasons for my conversion" lists first "my wife's instinctive and definitive response to our Lady, who was clearly beckoning us to come to the Church".

4. As far as God is concerned, one religion is as good as another. So for us humans the choice of a religion is just a matter of personal preference and taste.

On this one I'm not going to say a word. I'll leave the answer to my friend Henry, a former Methodist minister, who now works in a Catholic parish in the Midwest.

"The first thing that attracted me to the Catholic Church was the authority of the Church. I was looking for a Church that was more than a personal preference, a Church that had a claim to truth and not just to being what I happened to want.

"As a Methodist minister I was used to using many traditional liturgical elements—the Lord's Prayer, the Apostles' and Nicene Creeds, the rite for Holy Communion—from a sense that our worship needed to be grounded in the tradition of the whole Church. But there was no doctrinal or liturgical authority in Methodism to tell me to do so. It was simply my own choice, which meant it wasn't tradition at all in the theological sense.

"A question occurred to me: As Methodists, what did we mean when in the Apostles' Creed we affirmed our belief in 'the Holy Catholic Church'? We didn't really mean anything at all, because we rejected the idea of the visible unity of the whole Church. It was a mere abstraction, even a tautology: all Christians are Christians.

"Yet I knew that the authors of the Creed meant something very specific by 'the Holy Catholic Church'. They meant that the Church is one body in one faith, guided by the Holy Spirit to teach truth infallibly. In fact, they meant the Catholic Church. I had known that ever since I was in seminary, but it took years longer before I drew the necessary conclusion from the fact. If the Christian faith is more than a human invention, then we have the faith on the authority of the Church, and to have authority the Church must be one body.

"So the authority of the Church led me to her unity, and I realized that both things, unity and authority, were necessary if the Church had any claim at all to teach truth. The authority that lay behind the Creed had still to be present. It didn't make sense to think that the Holy Spirit would have guided the Church for five hundred years and then let it be 'every man for himself' after that.

"There had to be one true Church still, and looked at from that point of view the Catholic Church was the only credible candidate. It was the only Church that had held to the whole historic Christian faith, both doctrinally and morally. The very clarity of Catholic beliefs and the fact that the Church wasn't about to change them were strong points in favor of Catholicism.

"About that time the Catechism of the Catholic Church came out. My wife and I said to each other, 'Wouldn't it be great to belong to a Church that can tell you what it believes like that?'

"From that point it followed that if the Catholic Church's beliefs about herself were true, then everything else she taught must be true. Unlike some Protestant converts, once I believed in the Church's authority to teach the truth, I didn't have a great problem with Mary or giving up *sola Scriptura*. What was necessary was to escape the relativism of liberal Protestantism—to believe that truth is both important and knowable and must be acted on."

Needless to say, he did.

5. The really important thing in religious terms is to have a personal relationship with God. I don't need the Church for that. The Bible is enough, and I can pray directly to God whenever I want.

Indeed, each of us can and should pray directly to God and have an intimate, personal relationship with him, very much as a child does with his father. Each of us also can and should read and meditate on and pray over the Bible. But it is part of the terrible dynamic of fragmentation apparently built into Protestantism to suggest that in the final analysis all anybody needs are the Bible and private prayer.

For fifteen hundred years of Christianity it never occurred to anyone to suggest that the Bible was enough by itself. And today, in my experience, many good people who have very nearly memorized the Bible come to the Catholic

Church precisely because they want to hear God's authentic word spoken with authority there.

In fact, the Bible itself, both the Old and New Testaments, makes it perfectly clear that God formed his followers and disciples into a people—the People of God, who are the Church. Being a member of that Church is part of what having a personal relationship with God means and requires.

Consider the implications of St. Paul's image of the Church as the Body of Christ and of striking statements like this: "We, though many, are one body in Christ, and individually members of one another" (Rom 12:5). Being a member necessarily involves life with others in the community of faith and participation in the liturgical prayer of the community, above all the Eucharist, as well as the private conversation with God that we call personal prayer.

One of the most impressive testimonies I've encountered to the importance of membership in the Church comes from a young woman who wrote, "I fell in love with Catholicism because it has to be *real*. For Catholics, the Eucharist has to be the Real Presence of Christ. A living, breathing man must have spread his arms on a tree and let them be nailed in place on a particular date in history. That same risen Lord must be on the altar at every single Mass. It has to be *real*. These things are not up for debate or speculation, nor do they add up to some sort of moral allegory that merely gives us good example to follow.

"That's not the case for a Protestant. Yes, God exists, and, yes, we should all lead ethical lives. Beyond that, worship however you please, and we'll all get together in heaven. I came to reject the Protestant understanding because I realized faith is about more than living ethically. It is primarily about getting at the truth about things."

IX

Put Out into the Deep

The questions and objections in the last chapter had mainly to do with the Church—her doctrines, her structures and institutions, things like that. Other common issues about becoming Catholic touch on personal matters in the lives of some of those who find themselves attracted to Catholicism yet are concerned lest the leap into the Catholic Church be too hard and too painful for them.

Problems like these are often very real and agonizing. In dealing with them, proofs and arguments will take you just so far. Then something else has got to come into play: your own prayer and mortification, along with—and above all else—the action of God's grace. Let me repeat that so there will be no misunderstanding: someone who is interested in helping a friend find his way into the Catholic Church must be prepared to pray and do mortification—and ultimately must leave everything in the hands of God. A few lunches and a little apologetics won't get the job done.

That said, let's start with a fairly common objection that is not so personally excruciating as some.

1. I went to a Catholic Mass, and I found it incomprehensible and cold. I like a worship service that has some life and feeling in it.

Me, too. But remember that for someone who doesn't know the rules of baseball or chess, a ballgame or a chess match is no less incomprehensible than that Mass was to you. People can and do learn to understand and love all of them.

The Mass is, in a very real sense, the reason why the Church exists, both her origin and her purpose. It is, in famous words of the Second Vatican Council, "the summit toward which the activity of the Church is directed" and "the fount from which all her power flows" (Constitution on the Sacred Liturgy, 10). Many of the Protestant and Jewish converts I've worked with have been hungry for authentic worship, and they found it in the Catholic Mass even when the liturgical celebrations left something to be desired. Often I've had to caution such people not to receive Jesus in Communion as they were eager to do.

If someone finds it hard to understand and relate to the Mass, suggest that he read carefully through one of the missals (or missalettes) found in most churches. This attentive reading will help the person get an overview of the liturgy. Offer to attend Mass with this friend or relative, provide an explanation of what is going to happen in advance, and invite questions afterward. (If you feel a little uneasy about having to respond to questions, do some brushing up first.)

A man who, during a visit to a monastery months earlier, had begun to dabble with the idea of Catholicism records a fairly common sequence of events when he writes, "I went to Mass for the sake of our children, because my lapsed Catholic wife thought it would be good for them. And there I realized that the spark I had felt at the monastery was more at home in this building—an ugly modern church in the suburbs—than anywhere else. I kept on going. And soon I began the conversations that led to my conversion."

And another: "I attended Mass regularly and yearned to take the Body and Blood. I found myself dreaming of the day when I could. I started spending time before the Blessed Sacrament and was overcome with feelings I cannot adequately describe, but which kept drawing me closer and closer to Christ and his Church—and his Mother."

One last thought concerning the "problem" of the Mass.

The Catholic Mass is not a form of entertainment. It is worship. The validity and value of the Mass are not based on the music or the surroundings or the subjective feelings of the people in attendance. And although a good, well-preached homily is an excellent thing, the grace poured into hearts through the Eucharist does not depend on the oratorical skills of the priest but on the sacrificial action of Christ made present for our nourishment in Communion.

2. The Catholic Church has a lot to say about sex, and most of what she says is "no". How can anybody possibly live like that in this day and age?

Speaking of original sin, the famous twentieth century American Lutheran theologian Reinhold Niebuhr once remarked that this was the only empirically verifiable doctrine in Christianity. Whether original sin is the *only* such doctrine I couldn't say, but that it's empirically verifiable I have no doubt.

One of the saddest things I've read in a long time was the *New York Times*' obituary of French novelist Françoise Sagan. She was an enormously successful writer whose precocious first novel, *Bonjour Tristesse*, was a tremendous hit when it appeared in 1954. After that rousing start she published a long string of successful books and made a great deal of money along the way.

The *Times* obituary appeared on September 25, 2004. Here is the final paragraph:

"In a 1993 interview before her second drug trial, Ms. Sagan recalled: 'I had incredible luck because just when I grew up the pill came along. When I was 18, I used to die with fear of being pregnant, but then it arrived, and love was free and without consequence for nearly 30 years. Then AIDS came. Those 30 years coincided with my adulthood, the age for having fun.' "

Oh, what fun she must have had! Twice married, twice divorced, twice convicted of narcotics offenses, Ms. Sagan—who on one occasion suffered a fractured skull in the smashup of her expensive sports car—also said, "I believe I have a right to destroy myself as long as it does not harm anyone. If I feel like swallowing a glass of caustic soda, that's my problem."

No doubt Françoise Sagan's attitudes and behavior had other causes over and above the fact that she insisted on having so much "fun" in her own peculiar way. But can anyone seriously doubt that the lifestyle of sexual permissiveness was part of the self-destructive syndrome that marked her life?

For a long time secular culture has been in denial about matters having to do with sex. Françoise Sagan—God rest her soul!—was just one conspicuous case.

Human sexuality is a great and beautiful gift from God. But the residue of sin in human beings—both original sin and personal sin—makes the sexual drive more or less difficult to control and to order to the good ends of procreation and love. In order to exercise sexual self-control, we need God's grace and the virtue of chastity, which is an aspect or subcategory of the cardinal virtue of temperance.

Back in the fourth century, St. Augustine understood quite well what it meant to want and not want to be chaste. He called it "a sickness of the soul to be so weighted down by custom that [the soul] cannot wholly rise even with the support of truth". But persistent efforts to be chaste are eventually crowned with success. With God's help, Augustine succeeded. Later he wrote that as charity increases, "lust diminishes; when it reaches perfection, lust is no more." Good love drives out bad.

It *can* be done. It is eminently worth doing. And it is absolutely required that someone who wishes to become a Catholic make the effort to do it. "The Church restricts only about 2 percent of our behavior", one of my converts remarks. Yes, but it's a crucial 2 percent.

A woman whom I'll call Gwen sheds some surprising light on these matters in the account of her conversion.

Gwen was an upper-middle-class woman living in an upper-middle-class suburb of a large East Coast city. She was, she recalls, "rooted in the comfort zone of the 'ascendant Protestant' and the 'medium-high' Episcopal Church. This is a very comfortable place to be. It includes the perceived virtues of Planned Parenthood. The Catholic Church's stand on birth control and abortion is not even amusing, simply ignorant and harmful."

All the same, Gwen had persevered in instruction and was nearing the point of being received into the Church. The priest who was helping her pointed out that she would have to go to confession. That was something she dreaded. "What to confess?" she asked herself. "I was a virtuous person—and I shared the same feelings about birth control as my Catholic friends." I think we can guess what those feelings were.

The priest also told her that she needed a Catholic godparent. "Since my best Catholic friend was in Europe," Gwen says, "I called Hattie."

Hattie was a sixty-something black woman from Alabama. Abused by her family as a child, she'd found refuge in a convent of Catholic nuns. She became a Catholic, and in due course the nuns sent her north to work as a housekeeper and cook. "She became a treasure in our community", Gwen says. "Almost everyone had a Hattie story. That she was a black Catholic only made her more unusual in a very Protestant circle."

So Gwen called Hattie and asked her to meet her at the Catholic church after dinner and be her sponsor.

"She agreed", Gwen continues. "And then she asked if I felt ready to become a Catholic. That seemed a strange question. After all, Father seemed very comfortable with my decision. Nevertheless, I told her of my discomfort about the confession I had to make. I mentioned some of the questions in the little booklet I'd been given called *How to Make a Good Confession*. It actually mentioned birth control and other Stone Age ideas about morality.

"Instead of agreeing with me, Hattie said, 'Well, Mrs. Wheeler, it would seem to me that you're not a person who can live as a good Catholic, and you'd probably be happier not becoming one.'

"My first response was dead silence. Finally I reminded her to be at the church by seven and stand with me as my sponsor.

"That was the night I leaped off a cliff, not really knowing where I would land. My heart—not my mind—felt the strong desire to go somewhere I'd never been.

"Where I landed was more real and more glorious than anything I'd ever known."

To which I'll add only that I wish we had a lot more Hatties in the Church.

3. I was born and raised a Catholic, but I don't practice anymore. I'm in what the Church regards as a bad second marriage, and I know my first marriage can't be annulled—and I certainly have no intention of leaving my spouse.

In working with converts, I've yet to find a marriage problem that couldn't eventually be solved in a manner fully consistent with the teaching of the Church. And that includes people who have been involved in as many as three marriages.

But I don't mean to sound like Pollyanna. Not every story has a happy ending according to secular ideas about what "happy endings" must be like. Sacrifice and pain are part of everyone's life. They may play a large part indeed in the lives of people in "bad" marriages who want to be reconciled with the Church.

What do you tell a Catholic in this position? Something along these lines: "Unfortunately, your situation is very common these days. I have no instant guaranteed no-fail answers for you, but it's clear what you need to do.

"First of all, keep going to Mass every Sunday, without receiving Communion. Participate in other parish worship as well. No matter what happens, don't lose your faith.

"Second, talk it over with your pastor and listen closely to his advice.

"Third, bear in mind that, as the saying goes, 'it ain't over till it's over.' The Church wants you to return to full communion, even though it may not happen until near the end of your life.

"Do everything you can to bring your present marriage partner back to the Church or into the Church, as the case may be.

"Continue to acknowledge the validity and indissolubility of your first marriage. Make no excuses. Don't look for any shortcuts. Keep praying and trust in God. If we truly wish to be saved, there are very few limits to God's saving mercy."

4. I'm in a long-term relationship with someone I'm not married to. There is no possibility of our marrying, and I'm not going to give the relationship up.

If someone says that to you in the context of a religious discussion, it may be a sign that this person is starting to have second thoughts about his present way of life and is getting defensive as a result. Don't push or threaten, but encourage prayer, Scripture reading, and asking God for light. Grace may already be at work.

It goes without saying that someone who is really in love should want only what is best for the beloved. But if their relationship is not consonant with the teaching of Christ, it isn't "best" for the other party—it's worst. If you know someone in this situation who wants to open up to you, be prepared to listen and keep listening—and praying and mortifying yourself for that person, as long as it takes.

5. I guess it would be a good thing to be a Catholic, but my life has been such a sinful mess that I couldn't possibly live up to the obligations of membership in the Church.

Jesus insisted that he had come to save sinners, not the self-righteous. And God the Father didn't send his Son to die on the Cross for sinners without having the most difficult cases in mind. None of us lives up to the great gift we've been given—we all remain long-term, repetitious sinners right up to the moment of death, prodigal sons and daughters constantly returning to our compassionate Father.

The Church finds her model here, constantly offering people mercy and forgiveness through the sacraments, including baptism, penance, and even the anointing of the sick. Anyone who thinks he doesn't need this help is sadly mistaken.

And anyone who thinks he is *beyond* being helped either is making excuses for remaining in sin or else is guilty of a strange, inverted kind of pride. One of the people whom I received into the Church was personally responsible for tens of thousands of abortions. Do I hear someone out there who can claim to have done worse than that? Yet this man knew that, thanks to the mercy of God and the redemptive work of Christ, all that guilt was washed away in the saving waters of baptism.

In the magazine interview I mentioned earlier, Larry Kudlow recalled his own long, difficult struggle with alcohol and drugs. At one point, he said, "The roof fell down on my life." But he also recalled what I had told him—and would tell anybody else.

"Father John explained to me and taught me that Christ died for me as well as the rest of mankind. That I could identify with him personally. It was okay for me to use Christ as an example personally. Over time, he explained to me that my recovery from alcoholism and cocaine was part of Christ's redemption. I knew somehow that first of all, Christ wanted me to recover, and secondly, Christ would stand with me."

And of his baptism he says, "After the water was poured on me, I absolutely broke down and bawled my head off."

Larry Kudlow isn't alone. Confession? A convert named Don, whom I've mentioned earlier, speaks for many when he says, "Confession is a challenge because pride still abounds. I don't like to talk about my faults. I don't like to confront the reality of my sinfulness, especially where that sin is willfully committed.

"But confession has also been a great gift, a cleansing for my soul, a lifting of my burden. I always feel much better after confession, even if I don't feel good about it going in."

6. My wife (or husband—or parents or children) would be very upset if I became a Catholic.

Unfortunately, that's pretty common.

"I knew my family would not receive the news well." "It is extremely scary to convert, and I knew full well that my family would be stunned, disbelieving, and doubtful.

I would open myself to gossip, lose some friends, and be dismissed as having a midlife crisis." "The hardest part of converting is the rude, argumentative people who cannot handle the idea that I left." "When I first broke the subject of my conversion to my father, he swallowed his horror—for the moment. He gave it full vent later."

I've heard these things many times. No doubt there are more delicate ways of putting it, but the real answer has got to be so what? A person who wants to become a Catholic but is aware of the opposition of family or friends simply must bite the bullet, accept the fact that nothing can be done about it directly, and then forge ahead.

The best advice I can give anyone in this position is this: "Point out that your conscientious decision deserves respect, that the family members or friends in question have no right at all to give you a hard time, that becoming a Catholic doesn't mean you will love them any less, that this opposition is a form of bigotry. And then, having done all that, do what you know God wants you to do—come into the Catholic Church."

Almost universally, I've found that even the most recalcitrant family members come to accept the idea that one of their own has become a Catholic. Love and family ties see to that. It may take longer with friends and acquaintances, but if the new convert goes out of his way to keep up a relationship, friendship is likely to win out.

I have plenty of stories, by the way, illustrating how the conversion of one person can eventually help bring others—husbands, wives, children, parents, friends—into the Church. A man ends the note promising to send me his conversion story with this postscript: "Amanda"—his wife—"will be received into the Church June 22." It's not unusual.

Often, it seems, relatives and friends observe that the only visible change in a recent convert is a change for the better.

I frequently hear how much more affectionate, understanding, forgiving, and relaxed the new Catholic has become since the great event. It stands to reason. Someone who falls in love with Christ and embraces the faith remains a sinner with all the usual defects, but he has begun to love more—and it's noticed.

But let me conclude this brief treatment of the opposition that converts sometimes come up against with the strange and wonderful story of Linda, who began as part of the opposition herself.

"It really started when my daughter Gretchen decided to convert. I was furious. Especially I was furious with her high school Latin teacher, Dave McCoy, who had deeply influenced her. I was afraid she was being maneuvered into doing what she'd been told instead of thinking for herself.

"So I made an appointment to see Dave McCoy, and I told him in no uncertain terms to back off. I wouldn't leave until he agreed.

"Now, this is where it gets weird.

"God wouldn't let it end there. I was a pretty perfunctory Protestant, but I did believe in God, and I believed—as I believe now—that he communicates with me. What he said was, 'Oh, no. You aren't going to get away with it this time.'

"So I apologized to Dave McCoy in an effort to appease that voice, but I couldn't get McCoy out of my mind. Finally I began a very tentative e-mail correspondence with him. And as soon as I did, I understood with absolute clarity that I was being offered a choice by God.

"Either I could accept God on his terms—which I understood to mean becoming a Catholic—or I could walk away. And in walking away, I'd be shutting the door on God for the rest of my life.

"I never could explain it any better than that. I had no knowledge of Catholicism. I didn't know that God was a triune God or that Sunday Mass was an obligation. But within two weeks I knew I had to convert. It wasn't what Dave McCoy said that counted but what God offered.

"My difficulties were enormous, excruciating, exhausting. I was forty-nine and very aware of the impact this conversion would have on my loving family. I didn't want to convert. I loved my life as a Protestant and didn't want to lose it. I simply knew I had to make a choice: either accept God or walk away.

"On the plus side, I have a loving and supportive husband, despite his utter confusion about faith. And I had a good and humble parish priest to help me. But I had to become very humble to become a Catholic.

"Take one example. Even though I'd been baptized as a baby, my priest wouldn't accept that, and I had to go through a full baptism again. I vacillated. Three days before the baptism I wrote you in panic. You wrote back, 'I am here for you, Linda, but I will not push you over the edge.' That was absolutely the right thing to say. I wrote back, 'Thank you, and I am not writing again until the baptism happens.' Now I had the strength to face it on my own, as I absolutely had to do—the choice had to be mine, had to be between God and me.

"That was the conversion. It certainly is not the end of the story."

It never is. Not for Linda or for anyone else who at some point in the journey of his life seriously decides to do what is necessary to know, love, and serve God above everything else and to go wherever God wants and do whatever God wants done in order to accomplish that.

Those of us who are fortunate enough already to be Catholics know what that means. It means embracing the Catholic faith, entering into the communion of the Catholic

Church, becoming a Catholic Christian disciple of Jesus Christ and living accordingly.

It is a huge privilege to be able to help people respond to God's grace and make this decision. And it also is a responsibility, a serious obligation, for every member of the Church, including every Catholic lay person.

People who are well instructed in the faith and practicing it in a serious way are already prepared to be apostles. Yes, being an apostle and doing apostolate will always require more growth in knowledge and grace. But the time to get started is now, and the place to begin is right here—in the family, neighborhood, school or job or social setting where you presently find yourself and with the family members, friends, fellow workers, classmates, and associates you've got.

You are called to this work by your baptism. The Lord is speaking directly, personally to *you* when he says, "Put out into the deep and let down your nets for a catch."

In the fifth chapter of Luke's Gospel we read that Simon Peter, James, and John did as Jesus told them and had a great catch (cf. Lk 5:4–11). "And when they had brought their boats to land, they left everything and followed him."

This is a wonderful moment. The dawn starting to break after our long night of confusion, scandal, and dissent will be the greatest era in the history of the Catholic Church. We are called—every single one of us—to have full, active roles in the new evangelization that will build a civilization of truth and love. May our Blessed Mother Mary, Mother of the Church and Mother of the New Evangelization, lead us all safely to her Son.

APPENDIX

Catholic Lifetime Reading Plan

Compiled by
Father C. John McCloskey III

Adam, Karl. *The Spirit of Catholicism*. New York: Herder and Herder, 1997.

Alphonsus de Liguori. *Uniformity with God's Will*. Rockford, Ill.: TAN, 1977.

Augustine. *City of God*. New York: Doubleday, 1958.

———. *Confessions*. New York: Doubleday, 1960.

Aumann, Jordan. *Spiritual Theology*. London: Sheed, 1980.

Baur, Benedict. *Frequent Confession*. Princeton, N.J.: Scepter, 1999.

———. *In Silence with God*. Princeton, N.J.: Scepter, 1997.

Belloc, Hilaire. *The Great Heresies*. Rockford, Ill.: TAN, 1991.

———. *How the Reformation Happened*. Rockford, Ill.: TAN, 1992.

———. *Survivals and New Arrivals*. Rockford, Ill.: TAN, 1993.

Benson, Robert Hugh. *Lord of the World*. South Bend, Ind.: St. Augustine's, 2001.

Bernanos, Georges. *The Diary of a Country Priest*. New York: Carroll and Graf, 2002.

Bouyer, Louis. *Spirit and Forms of Protestantism*. Princeton, N.J.: Scepter, 2001.

Boylan, Eugene. *Difficulties in Mental Prayer*. Princeton, N.J.: Scepter, 2001.

———. *This Tremendous Lover*. Allen, Tex.: Ave Maria, 1987.

Burke, Cormac. *Covenanted Happiness: Love and Commitment in Marriage*. 2nd ed. Princeton, N.J.: Scepter Publications, 1999.

Carroll, Warren H. *A History of Christendom*. Vol. 1: *The Founding of Christendom*. Front Royal, Va.: Christendom College, 1985.

———. *A History of Christendom*. Vol. 2: *The Building of Christendom*. Front Royal, Va.: Christendom College, 1987.

———. *A History of Christendom*. Vol. 3: *The Glory of Christendom*. Front Royal, Va.: Christendom Press, 1993.

———. *A History of Christendom*. Vol. 4: *The Cleaving of Christendom*. Front Royal, Va.: Christendom College, 2000.

Catechism of the Catholic Church. 2nd ed. Vatican City: Libreria Editrice Vaticana, 1994, 1997, 2000.

Catherine of Siena. *Little Talks with God*. Brewster, Mass.: Paraclete, 2001.

Caussade, Jean-Pierre de. *Abandonment to Divine Providence*. New York: Doubleday, 1975.

Cervantes, Miguel de. *Don Quixote*. New York: Oxford University Press, 1998.

Chautard, Jean-Baptiste. *Soul of the Apostolate*. Rockford, Ill.: TAN, 1946.

Chesterton, Gilbert Keith. *The Everlasting Man*. San Francisco: Ignatius, 1993.

———. *Orthodoxy*. San Francisco: Ignatius, 1995.

———. *St. Thomas Aquinas; St. Francis of Assisi*. San Francisco: Ignatius, 2002.

Covey, Stephen R. *The Seven Habits of Highly Effective People: Restoring the Character Ethic*. New York: Simon and Schuster, 2003.

Crocker, Harry. *Triumph: The Power and the Glory of the Catholic Church*. New York: Random House, 2003.

Dante. *The Divine Comedy*. New York: Random House, 1959; New York: Knopf, 1995.

Dawson, Christopher. *Christianity and European Culture: Selections from the Work of Christopher Dawson*. Washington, D.C.: Catholic University of America, 1998.

Day, Dorothy. *The Long Loneliness: The Autobiography of Dorothy Day*. New York: HarperCollins, 1997.

Eliot, Thomas Stearns. *Christianity and Culture*. Orlando, Fla.: Harcourt, 1990.

Endo, Shusaku. *Silence*. Marlboro, N.J.: Taplinger, 1980.

Escriva, Josemaria. *Christ Is Passing By: Homilies*. Princeton, N.J.: Scepter, 2002.

———. *Friends of God: Homilies*. Princeton, N.J.: Scepter, 2002.

———. *The Way, Furrow, the Forge*. Princeton. N.J.: Scepter, 2001.

———. *The Way of the Cross*. Princeton, N.J.: Scepter, 1999.

Faber, Frederick. *All for Jesus*. Rockford, Ill.: TAN, 1991.

Francis de Sales. *Introduction to the Devout Life*. New York: Doubleday, 1972.

———. *Treatise on the Love of God*. Rockford, Ill.: TAN, 1997.

Garrigou-Lagrange, Reginald. *The Three Ages of the Interior Life*. Rockford, Ill.: TAN, 1999.

Guardini, Romano. *End of the Modern World*. Wilmington, Del.: Intercollegiate Studies Institute, 1998.

———. *The Lord*. Washington, D.C.: Regnery, 2002.

Hahn, Scott, and Kimberly Hahn. *Rome Sweet Home: Our Journey to Catholicism*. San Francisco: Ignatius, 1993.

Hopkins, Gerard Manley. *Hopkins: Poetry and Prose*. New York: Knopf, 1995.

John XXIII. *Journal of a Soul: The Autobiography of Pope John XXIII*. New York: Doubleday, 1999.

John of the Cross. *Dark Night of the Soul*. New York: Doubleday, 1990. Also in *The Collected Works of John of the Cross*. Trans. Kieran Kavanaugh, O.C.D., and Otilio Rodriguez, O.C.D. Washington, D.C.: Institute of Carmelite Studies, 1973.

John Paul II. *Crossing the Threshold of Hope*. New York: Knopf, 1995.

Knox, Ronald. *Enthusiasm: A Chapter in the History of Religion*. Notre Dame, Ind.: University of Notre Dame, 1994.

Kreeft, Peter. *Christianity for Modern Pagans: Pascal's* Pensées *Edited, Outlined and Explained*. San Francisco: Ignatius, 1993.

Leclercq, Jean. *Love of Learning and the Desire for God: A Study of Monastic Culture*. New York: Fordham University, 2003.

Lewis, Clive Staples. *Mere Christianity*. New York: HarperCollins, 2001.

———. *The Problem of Pain.* New York: HarperCollins, 2001.

———. *The Screwtape Letters.* New York: HarperCollins, 2001.

Louis de Granada. *Sinner's Guide.* Rockford, Ill.: TAN, 1983.

Louis Grignion de Montfort. *True Devotion to Mary.* Rockford, Ill.: TAN, 1985.

Lovasik, Lawrence. *The Hidden Power of Kindness: A Practical Handbook for Souls Who Dare to Transform the World, One Deed at a Time.* Manchester, N.H.: Sophia, 1999.

Manzoni, Alessandro. *The Betrothed.* London: Penguin, 1972.

Martinez, Luis. *True Devotion to the Holy Spirit.* Manchester, N.H.: Sophia, 2000.

Masson, Georgina. *Companion Guide to Rome.* New York: Boydell and Brewer, 2003.

Merton, Thomas. *The Seven Storey Mountain.* Orlando, Fla.: Harcourt, 1999.

Monti, James. *The King's Good Servant but God's First: The Life and Writings of St. Thomas More.* San Francisco: Ignatius, 1997.

More, Thomas. *The Sadness of Christ.* Princeton, N.J.: Scepter, 1997.

Muggeridge, Malcolm. *Something Beautiful for God.* New York: Harper and Row, 1986.

Newman, John Henry. *Apologia pro Vita Sua.* New York: Dover, 2005.

———. *Essay on the Development of Christian Doctrine.* Notre Dame, Ind.: University of Notre Dame, 1989.

———. *Idea of a University.* Notre Dame, Ind.: University of Notre Dame, 1982.

———. *Parochial and Plain Sermons.* San Francisco: Ignatius, 1997.

O'Connor, Flannery. *Collected Works.* New York: Library of America, 1988.

Ott, Ludwig. *Fundamentals of Catholic Dogma.* Rockford, Ill.: TAN, 1974.

Oursler, Fulton. *The Greatest Story Ever Told.* New York: Doubleday, 1989.

Percy, Walker. *Lost in the Cosmos: The Last Self-Help Book.* New York: Picador, 2000.

———. *Love in the Ruins.* New York: Picador, 1999.

Perquin, Bonaventure. *Abba Father*. Princeton, N.J.: Scepter, 2001.
Pieper, Josef. *The Four Cardinal Virtues*. Notre Dame, Ind.: University of Notre Dame, 1966.
Rice, Charles. *Fifty Questions on the Natural Law*. San Francisco: Ignatius, 1999.
Rohrbach, Peter. *Conversation with Christ*. Rockford, Ill.: TAN, 1994.
Scupoli, Lorenzo. *Spiritual Combat*. Manchester, N.H.: Sophia, 2002.
Sertillanges, A. G. *The Intellectual Life: Its Spirit, Conditions, Methods*. Washington, D.C.: Catholic University of America, 1987.
Sheed, Frank. *Theology and Sanity*. San Francisco: Ignatius, 1993.
———. *Theology for Beginners*. Cincinnati: St. Anthony Messenger, 1981.
Sheen, Fulton. *Life of Christ*. New York: Doubleday, 1990.
———. *Three to Get Married*. Princeton, N.J.: Scepter, 1996.
Sienkiewicz, Henry. *Quo Vadis*. Washington, D.C.: Regnery, 1998.
Stein, Edith. *Woman*. Washington, D.C.: Institute of Carmelite Studies, 1998.
Suarez, Federico. *Mary of Nazareth*. Princeton, N.J.: Scepter, 2003.
Tanquerey, Adolphe. *The Spiritual Life: A Treatise on Ascetical and Mystical Theology*. Rockford, Ill.: TAN, 2000.
Teresa, Mother. *Meditations from a Simple Path*. New York: Random House, 1996.
Teresa of Avila. *The Interior Castle*. New York: Doubleday, 1989. Also in *The Collected Works of St. Teresa of Avila*. Vol. 2. Washington, D.C.: Institute of Carmelite Studies, 1980.
———. *The Way of Perfection*. New York: Doubleday, 2004. Also in *The Collected Works of St. Teresa of Avila*. Vol. 2. Washington, D.C.: Institute of Carmelite Studies, 1980.
Thérèse of Lisieux. *The Story of a Soul*. Washington, D.C.: Institute of Carmelite Studies, 1996.
Thomas à Kempis. *The Imitation of Christ*. New York: Doubleday, 1989; San Francisco: Ignatius, 2005.
Thomas Aquinas. *My Way of Life*. Brooklyn, N.Y.: Confraternity of the Precious Blood, 1952.
Tolkien, John Ronald Reuel. *The Lord of the Rings*. New York: Houghton-Mifflin, 1994.

Trochu, François. *The Cure of Ars*. Rockford, Ill.: TAN, 1977.

Undset, Sigrid. *Kristin Lavransdatter*. Vol. 1: *The Wreath*. New York: Penguin, 1997.

———. *Kristin Lavransdatter*. Vol. 2: *The Wife*. New York: Penguin, 1999.

———. *Kristin Lavransdatter*. Vol. 3: *The Cross*. New York: Penguin, 2000.

von Hildebrand, Dietrich. *Transformation in Christ: On the Christian Attitude*. San Francisco: Ignatius, 2001.

Walsh, William. *Our Lady of Fatima*. New York: Doubleday, 1954.

Waugh, Evelyn. *Brideshead Revisited*. New York: Little, Brown, 1999.

Wegemer, Gerard. *Thomas More: A Portrait of Courage*. Princeton, N.J.: Scepter, 1997.

Weigel, George. *Witness to Hope: The Biography of Pope John Paul II*. New York: Harper Collins, 2001.